Best New Games

Updated Edition

Dale N. Le Fevre, MA

Director, New Games International
and Playworks

Human Kinetics

Library of Congress Cataloging-in-Publication Data

Le Fevre, Dale N.
  Best new games / Dale N. Le Fevre. -- Updated ed.
     p. cm.
  Includes bibliographical references.
  ISBN-13: 978-1-4504-2188-1 (soft cover)
  ISBN-10: 1-4504-2188-1 (soft cover)
1. Games. 2. Educational games. I. Title.
  GV1201.L453 2012
  790.1--dc23
                              2011045622

ISBN-10: 1-4504-2188-1 (print)
ISBN-13: 978-1-4504-2188-1 (print)

The web addresses cited in this text were current as of February 10, 2012, unless otherwise noted.

Acquisitions Editor: Cheri Scott; **Managing Editor:** Amy Stahl; **Assistant Editor:** Rachel Brito; **Copyeditor:** Jan Feeney; **Permissions Manager:** Dalene Reeder; **Graphic Designer:** Joe Buck; **Graphic Artist:** Denise Lowry; **Cover Designer:** Keith Blomberg; **DVD Face Designer:** Susan Rothermel Allen; **Photographer (cover):** © Human Kinetics; **Photographer (interior):** John Birchard, unless otherwise noted. Photo on page 12 by Sverre Koxvold, photos on pages 61 and 97 by Dale Le Fevre, and photos on page 98 and 99 by Sophie Hunter; **Photo Production Manager:** Jason Allen; **Art Manager:** Kelly Hendren; **Associate Art Manager:** Alan L. Wilborn; **Illustrations:** © Human Kinetics; **Printer:** United Graphics

We thank First Baptist Church at Savoy in Savoy, Illinois, for assistance in providing the location for the video shoot for this book.

Printed in the United States of America   10 9 8 7 6 5 4 3 2 1

The paper in this book is certified under a sustainable forestry program.

Human Kinetics
Website: www.HumanKinetics.com

United States: Human Kinetics, P.O. Box 5076, Champaign, IL 61825-5076
800-747-4457
e-mail: humank@hkusa.com

Canada: Human Kinetics, 475 Devonshire Road Unit 100, Windsor, ON N8Y 2L5
800-465-7301 (in Canada only)
e-mail: info@hkcanada.com

Europe: Human Kinetics, 107 Bradford Road, Stanningley, Leeds LS28 6AT, United Kingdom
+44 (0) 113 255 5665
e-mail: hk@hkeurope.com

Australia: Human Kinetics, 57A Price Avenue, Lower Mitcham, South Australia 5062
08 8372 0999
e-mail: info@hkaustralia.com

New Zealand: Human Kinetics, P.O. Box 80, Torrens Park, South Australia 5062
0800 222 062
e-mail: info@hknewzealand.com

E5621

Dedicated to my stepchildren, Clare, Tom, and Peter;
and Hannah and Robert.
Also dedicated to my teacher, Sogyal Rinpoche.

You may be disappointed if you fail, but you are doomed if you don't try.
—Beverly Sills

Every exit is an entry somewhere else.
—Tom Stoppard

Laughter is the sun that drives the winter from the human face.
—Victor Hugo

Contents

Preface

New Games provide a situation where all participants can share a common sense of joy. That is what makes New Games remarkable.

  —Dale N. Le Fevre

If anyone were to ask me if I believe miracles happen, my answer would have to be "All the time!" For me, finding New Games is one great example. Having just left my previous job, I was looking for something I loved doing. I happened to catch a TV show called *Make A Wish* with a feature on New Games. I sat riveted; when the clip finished, I proclaimed my wish: "I want to do New Games!"

I called the TV station, spoke to the show producer, who told me the address of New Games and I wrote to them. After several months, I got a phone call. "Do you want to train with us?" the director of the New Games Foundation asked me. "Sure!" I replied, and a week and a long cross-country drive later in February 1975, I was in San Francisco ready to begin what has become my New Games career. Since that beginning, I have presented New Games in workshops all over North America and Europe (including Northern Ireland, Poland, Croatia, and Serbia), as well as in nations scattered throughout the world—Israel, South Africa, Japan, Australia, New Zealand, and India. I had wanted to travel, but I never expected anything like this! My wish had come true, and then some! My current fantasies are to go to Mongolia, China, Russia, and Antarctica to teach New Games.

The best career advice to give to the young is "Find out what you like doing best, then get someone to pay you for doing it."

  —Katherine Whitehorn

What makes New Games such a powerful experience that I could build a career by teaching them? First, New Games are one of the best ways known to break down barriers between people. While playing New Games, people who start as total strangers end as new friends. People who have known each other a long time see each other in a new light, deepening their relationships. Communication is opened up with these games. Team building is a natural consequence—it's easy to develop positive feelings for other participants. In the end, you want them to have fun as much as you do. Under such friendly circumstances, it is hard to maintain animosity.

Even when people don't speak the same language, New Games is a universal language that allows them to connect in a friendly way. While cooperative play may not be the answer to all the world's problems, it provides a joyous starting point for creating better relationships. I have taught New

Games to many mixed groups. Unbelievable as it may seem, even Arabs and Israelis in the Middle East; Catholics and Protestants in Northern Ireland during the "troubles"; mixed races in South Africa during apartheid; and Serbs, Croats, and Muslims in Croatia and Serbia (just after the shooting had stopped) were able to play the games and have fun together.

New Games can also help people relax and discover reservoirs of creativity and boldness they didn't know they had. The experience of New Games can build in participants the attitude of "Why not!" readying them for challenges they might not have been able to handle before. That has certainly been my experience. My New Games adventures have given me the confidence to tackle all kinds of new areas. Although I think of myself as a basically shy person, in the years since I began doing and teaching New Games, I have presented games to a group of several thousand; although I didn't (and still don't) know how to program my DVD player, I have produced six commercial videos, a CD-ROM, and four DVDs. Although I never wrote anything longer than a 24-page term paper (double spaced) in college, in my New Games career I have written three books, so far. Why not!

So what is a New Game? It is a cooperative group game that people do together and is done just for fun and is for everybody regardless of age, size, sex, or ability level. To be clear, this has nothing to do with video games or computers. The games sometimes include competition, but anybody can win. That's because when there is winning, it is only one element rather than *the* main element of a game. No trophies or awards are given for winning; we simply go on to another game. This way, everyone can play without having to suffer the extremes of competition. Instead of being eliminated, players change roles or sides and keep playing. And always, enjoying a New Game is more important than winning it. In this sense, everybody, whether a competitive or noncompetitive player, wins every game.

> *The important thing in life is not the victory but the contest;*
> *the essential thing is not to have won but to have fought well.*
>
> —Baron Pierre de Coubertin

This book is the most comprehensive written presentation of New Games currently available, with descriptions, pictures, guides on developmental skills, icebreakers, games to use to get acquainted, games to build sensitivity and trust, and games to promote team building. It also includes which games to start and finish with. There are sections on leading, adapting, and creating games. And more. In short, I have created this book to teach you the best New Games and how to present them. Further, there is a DVD which shows how to present and play several of the games. While you are not bound to this, it gives you a place to start from.

While there is much to glean from my experience, you may find, in a given situation, that doing something other than what I recommend works for you. Congratulations! Don't believe everything you read. Although advice based on my experience is generally very good, please feel free to ignore it and see what works for you.

Best New Games is a great resource for anyone involved with groups at any level and in any setting. It is a rich mine of entertaining activities for scout troops, elementary classes, afterschool programs, PE programs for all ages, college orientations, religious youth groups, retirement home residents, day care kids and adults, and park district programs. This book contains material for people planning parties; icebreakers for a conference or meeting; or activities for any group that includes people who are very different from one another in age, ability level, ethnicity, or culture. It demonstrates how to lead people of all ages and abilities in having fun together while being physically and mentally active.

> *There's an intrinsic value in doing something without being the best at it.*
>
> —*Susie Gephardt quoted by Susan McCullough in the* Washington Post

We begin with an indispensable chapter covering some of the basics of using the games, including a brief history of New Games, how to lead New Games, how to adapt games, and how to create games of your own. It is possible to lead the games presented without reading this chapter, but you will be a lot more likely to be successful at it if you gain the benefit of my experience outlined in chapter 1. Chapter 2 gives you a thorough listing of several countries' standards that are met by the New Games included in this book. Chapters 3 through 6 present games of various activity levels, from low to high. Chapter 7 is about trust games, which are done to deepen trust after some level of trust has already been established with a group. These chapters include instructions on playing each game as well as tips about number of participants, when to do the game, safety, accommodations for various age levels, space and equipment required, and developmental skills used. The activity level of each game is indicated by the chapter titles in the lower-right corner of every game.

In the afterword, I get the last word, including a personal story that illustrates perfectly the way I feel about New Games and the reason I want to share them with as many people as possible!

Acknowledgments

I would like to express my deep gratitude to the following:

Redwood School, Fort Bragg, California

Barbara Buell, principal, and all the teachers, students, staff, and parents at Redwood School

Wanda Windsor, pastor, and the youth group from the United Methodist Church, Fort Bragg

The Community School, Mendocino, California

The New Games Mentoring Class and friends, Fort Bragg

Kim Sanderson for his support of New Games concepts, Edmonton, Alberta, Canada

Wendy Moffatt for advice and help in editing

How to Use This Book and DVD

Or, where, when, and with whom these games can be used.

Elementary and Secondary Schools: In the Classroom

Certainly you thought of schoolchildren during free play, in youth clubs, and afterschool clubs. But I hope you didn't forget about schoolchildren while they're in the classroom learning languages, science, math, and almost any other subject. (A few of the games can be used just as they are, such as In the Manner of the Adverb and Bloomps; most of the games work with some degree of adaptation.) After all, learning is a lot more fun if you can play and learn at the same time. Studies have shown that students retain ideas and concepts better if they do something physical that captures their interest. It makes sense. Not only can you discuss what happens in the process of the game, but while you are playing the game, the ideas go into your body as well. Einstein claimed that he got the idea for relativity as a feeling in his muscles. We learn not only through our minds but with our bodies as well. (Some would maintain the spirit, too, and I would agree—but that is outside of the scope of this book.)

Further, research has shown that there is a relationship between physical activity and the release of endorphins in the brain, which enhance creativity and lead to learning. Why ignore an activity that engages students' interest while they acquire the learning skills of listening, concentrating, and following directions?

To Increase Fitness and Address Obesity

Most people would agree that children as well as adults in the West are becoming increasingly overweight and unfit. It seems that every month a new study comes out confirming this. How we eat is certainly a contributing factor, but so is our sedentary lifestyle. While some New Games do not require much movement, the majority have some degree of activity.

New Games are not a cure-all for obesity and fitness, but they do allow students (as well as teachers and playground personnel) who are normally left out of play and games an opportunity to join in. Participants don't think about doing the activities to control weight or keep fit—they play the games because they're fun. New Games just happen to make a difference to those not inclined to participate in sport or recreation games. I've seen this happen many times. I conducted a research project featuring New Games in order to see what effect they had on children. At the start, one overweight boy would constantly find excuses to sit out. We accepted that and allowed him to watch. After a while, he saw that he could actually take part without being embarrassed or made fun of, and by the end of the program he was participating fully and enthusiastically.

To Address Bullying

New Games give all participants various perspectives of themselves and each other. Everyone gets involved, leaving their normal role behind. People relate to each other in friendly and accepting ways that they otherwise would not consider. When all players are laughing and having fun together, it's hard to have negative feelings either way. Bullies and the bullied can relax because they are having a good time, and both are accepted and given respect through participating fully as members of the games, which under normal circumstances does not happen.

Colleges and Universities

Let's look at some areas that may not be obvious. At colleges and universities, take freshman orientation or new-student orientation. New Games give new or transferring students a chance to meet people when they most likely know no one or very few people, at best. Speaking from personal experience, starting this new venture can be scary. The games help everyone to relax and meet others under friendly and nonthreatening circumstances.

When I was a college freshman, one of the most fun things we did was a trust circle (referred to in this book as Wind in the Willows) that most everyone could play. This activity went on for quite some time and it really took the tension away, making me start to feel less apprehensive about moving away from home for the first time, starting what I expected to be incredibly hard courses, and being with a bunch of strangers. The physical contact in a safe setting really contributed to allowing me to feel accepted and at the same time comforted.

New Games courses can be taught as part of university curriculums, not only for physical education and recreation students (which is a natural link) but also as part of teacher education courses at the undergraduate and graduate levels. New Games have also been taught as continuing education courses for teachers and other adults. As economic cutbacks affect how many schools and school districts can have physical education programs, classroom teachers have been called on to take the lead in providing PE activities for their classes.

Many teachers led games with their students long before the budget cuts, however. It gives teachers a great way to connect with their students, which makes the learning process easier and more fun. And, as I've pointed out, you can teach many concepts using games as a metaphor. When kids actually get to do something while absorbing content, rather than sit and memorize facts, they really remember the lessons.

Businesses

Playing games with business people? At first it sounds incongruous, but games have become well established for team building. New Games in general don't have quite the same hard edge as traditional team-building exercises because they are played first for fun. After doing the initial games just for fun, however, you can employ games for the specific purpose of team building (and certain games are especially appropriate). Players have to cooperate in several of the games in order to make them work. It makes sense, after getting players to relax by playing just for fun, to use games as a way of studying the behavior and interactions of the whole group and individuals in the group. This can lead to better group work, but the games and the following discussion must be sensitively and properly led.

The game of Knots is a good example. While it allows everyone to touch in a safe way, thereby building trust, it requires people to think and be imaginative to get out of the knot. Further, afterwards the group can start by talking about what went on in the game—who came up with ideas, who felt listened to, who felt they weren't heard. At this point, people are relaxed from playing the game and talking; the next step for the presenter is to relate the game to the work experience. Is this like what happens at work? Or is it completely different, and how? For this to be effective, management has to be prepared to act on some (if not all) of the suggestions people come up with to improve operations. Otherwise, they will become frustrated and feel manipulated by the whole process.

In Meetings

There are other ways in which New Games can be used for business purposes, such as in meetings. Starting a meeting with a brief game can lighten the atmosphere so that participants relate to each other in a productive way. When the heaviness of the task at hand is lifted, workers do better work. The games also work well as revitalizers when the group's energy is flagging, and they're instrumental in getting creative juices flowing. The games call for imaginative input, and a skilled leader can channel that creativity into the work process and discussions.

At Conferences

New Games have been used often to open and close conferences. Immediately a relaxed atmosphere is established when opening a conference with a game. People who don't know each other and who appear nervous at the start of a game are friendly toward each other at the end. Every session afterward goes better when this initial mood is established. Suggestions of openers are made in the Game Finder in the "Appropriate social purposes" column. Which one to choose depends on your group, the space available, the number of participants, and the mood they're in. However, this is not the only way to use New Games at conferences. They can be used as energizers at any point when the attention level is flagging. Participants perk up after even one game. Also, the games are a great way to bring closure to the conference, letting people leave with a warm and fuzzy feeling.

For Social Events

Finally, businesses can take the more lighthearted approach to using the games for social gatherings and picnics. The activities create a good feeling and reduce inhibitions without having to resort to alcohol. Having fun together, perhaps even with whole families included, may be the best team builder of all!

Youth Groups

Many of the problems that affect schools affect youth groups as well: obesity, lack of fitness, and bullying. New Games are the best team-building activities and icebreaker games I've ever come across for youth groups. For one, everyone is included and gets to play as fully as they are prepared to do. The youth groups I joined as a kid usually presented games that were highly competitive. Less athletic kids and many of the girls felt left out or even embarrassed because they lacked the skills required of the games. Remember, this was a time when people thought girls should be, for the most part, not very athletic. Hence, generally speaking, they didn't practice very competitive games that much and so they were naturally not very good at them. This, as we have seen, has changed.

New Games are fun for youth groups because the games include both sexes fully. Also, players of all ages, sizes, and abilities are able to participate. It is not unusual in a game where there is competition for someone who never usually wins competitive games to win. I've seen it happen time and again. It might be because the fastest and strongest are actually targeted first to help catch the others. In any case, it's a pretty thrilling and unusual event for the person involved.

Even Teenagers Play New Games

As unlikely as it may seem, teens will play and enjoy these games. Okay, at first many may be skeptical. Even resistant. Perhaps totally noncompliant. They don't want to look uncool doing little kids' games. But once you get them past being cool, they'll play. The role of the presenter is to somehow get them to join, to give them permission to play. It may take a little coaxing.

One time I flew to Rochester, New York, to lead games with a group of about 50 teens in a gym. They all came in and sat down on the bleachers, and I was introduced. After a few words, I invited them down to do the games. Nobody moved. Immediately I sensed that my next words would make it or break it, so I just said something like this: "Look, I came an awful long way to be with you today. All I'm asking is to try one game. If you don't like it, then you can sit." I think they got that I was being honest with them, and they did come down to the floor, played the game enthusiastically, and kept playing for the hour I was with them.

It helps if leaders take part in the games, thereby showing a willingness to make fools of themselves. This increases the trust factor immensely. I always do this. After all, I love doing the games.

Religious Groups

It will be no surprise to you that kids in religious groups like the games as much as kids in any group. That's not at issue here.

One way of relating parables from religious texts that I've used is putting the story in the form of a game. While kids can study written or spoken stories, if the kids are like me, they won't forget those stories when they're presented as a game. Each child's interests are highly involved then, making the ideas offered engaging. It's not too difficult to use a game as it is or to adapt it to fit the story. And it's fun for the person telling the story as well.

Further, most religions are based on love, and I believe love is expressed by including those who are normally left out of activities because of their shortcomings—too big or small, too slow, lacking in skills, and those who are normally ostracized.

Mental Health Settings

Let me state for the record that New Games are not therapy. Having said that, I believe that playing the games can be therapeutic. I gave my very first New Games session with a group of autistic people many years ago. I didn't feel that the session went very well, since the group, other than their caregivers, did not participate much. I was feeling a little down about that when one of the staff came up to me and, putting things in perspective, exclaimed, "I've never seen Jerry even react to any of the activities we've done, even if he did many of them in his own way. Most of all, he smiled and laughed, which is a first! All of the folks were much more involved than in anything else we've ever done."

Physical and Occupational Therapy Settings

Again, New Games are not therapy, but I know physical and occupational therapists who use New Games to encourage movement and involvement in their groups. Clients are quite responsive to the games, and their ability to move and do certain physical actions is improved. Because the games engage their interests, the people are quite happy to take part.

Competitive Sport: Winning Is . . . Playing

New Games give those who love competition a respite from their usual "winning isn't everything; it's the only thing" mentality. We can all see what happens when that philosophy rules: Players injure other players, as long as it's within the rules. Brutality can help their team to win. So it becomes okay to dislocate a quarterback's arm in pro football or destroy a catcher's ankle on a slide home in baseball. In New Games, we don't have to suffer the extremes of competition. Players aren't eliminated; they change roles or even sides and can keep playing, if they want to. It's hard to build up animosity towards other players when you might be on their side or they on yours from one minute to the next.

There *is* competition in many New Games. It just doesn't matter who wins. This allows players to relax and enjoy the game. For many highly competitive people, this is like a breath of fresh air. But, as I once heard John O'Connell, former director of New Games, say, competition is like adding spice to food. If you don't have any, food tastes bland. Too much and it spoils the flavor.

What often happens is that players go after the biggest and best players to catch them first so that they can in turn help catch others. So the tiny kid is the last one caught and wins the game. I've seen this happen quite often. This is quite an experience for that kid, who maybe never won anything before.

Football and Me

One of the biggest surprises I encountered was during a tour to promote New Games in Sweden. I was contracted to present New Games throughout the country to youth football (soccer) clubs. My first sessions involved people of both sexes; as I correctly assumed, the stress on competition wasn't so strong and the games worked easily. But then I came to my first one that was all male, including their coaches. *Uh-oh,* I thought. They looked pretty rugged. It was in a rural area where I wasn't sure they would buy into the idea of cooperative New Games. I thought they'd never go for it, that they would think it was too silly or not get that there wasn't always a winner, or it doesn't matter who wins.

But, what the heck, I was getting paid. So I started the session with no idea of what would happen. To my delight, they played the games really hard and had a blast! This taught me two things: One, don't have too many expectations. Two, let people figure out for themselves how much fun it is to play New Games. All I can do is set things up for them to enjoy our time together. And of course have fun myself. Which I do.

Have You Thought Of . . .

Where can you use New Games? The short answer is with *any* group. But let's take a look at a few specific groups and how the games apply to them.

For Union Activity

Once I can remember some union organizers who came to my workshop to learn how to do the games as a way to unite their workers. They were thinking of doing the games with families at a picnic, but it is a great way to come together around divisive issues as well. If you assemble people and get them in a good mood and more familiar with each other in a friendly way, the group is more likely to work better together.

When Camping

While there are a number of games that work with a small group, you can get to enjoy your family and know fellow campers by inviting them to join in some New Games. It's a lot of fun and you'll feel friendlier toward your fellow campers. This might be obvious to you. But don't be afraid to try it. If, while you are playing the games, you notice someone looking on, interested, invite them to join. If it's a kid, you might want to ask the parents if it's okay with them.

In Your Neighborhood

A good way to get to know your neighbors is to have a party and invite them to join in some New Games. The adults might be willing to let their kids play, but after a game or two, bring the kids together in a huddle and ask them to invite their parents. More often than not, the parents do join, and, surprisingly to them, they have a ball. It gives them a way to relate to their kids that they might never have tried before, bringing them closer. It gives parents a chance to be childlike as well. In the end, not only will you get to know your neighbors better, but they'll get to know their own families better as well.

Every Group

I'm not going to try to name every group that these games could work with. I have highlighted only a few to give you an idea of where, when, and with whom to use New Games. I leave it to your imagination to determine how *you* can use the games with your group. So, as they say, the ball is in your court. What will you do with it?

New Games on DVD

A DVD is bound into the back of this book that will make it even easier for you to use the games. Although the games are well explained and the pictures are very descriptive in the book, it is a static medium. The DVD shows several games from the book being introduced to a group and shows what the games look like in action. The games highlighted on the DVD are noted in the book with a DVD icon in the Game Finder on pages xxiv to xxxiii and in the game descriptions, too. While the way you play them may end up different than what you see on the DVD, it does give you a starting point.

Game Finder

This section includes a game finder, which lays out the games under headings and will help you find the right game for a particular situation or help you plan a series of games for a session.

Using the Game Finder

Almost all of these games can be done with all ages, starting with age 3 and extending up into the 90s. Naturally, adaptations may be necessary. Such adaptations are highly individualistic and so they are not listed here, but special instructions are given in individual game descriptions. High-trust activities are listed at the end of the game finder.

Following are the headings for the game finder:

• **Activity level** lets you know just how much physical exertion it will take to play the game. Levels are as follows:

Low

Low/moderate

Moderate

High

• **When to play the game** tells you whether a game is particularly appropriate for the beginning, middle, or end of a play session. That does not mean that the game can't be played any other time, however, experience has proven its special suitability for the times indicated in the game finder. If the time slot identified is followed by [C], that means that game works especially well in that position for children. If it is followed by [A], it means that the game works especially well in that position for adults. "Any time" simply means that the game can be used any time in a play session.

When you are planning a games session, keep in mind that each game lasts approximately five minutes—and that it is better to have too many games planned than too few!

• **Number of players** reflects the range for the optimal number of players for that game to work well and ensure that everyone will have an opportunity to participate and have a good time.

• **Space and equipment needed** notes unusual requirements for space and what equipment (if any) is needed. Most games need at least room for a circle of players with no obstacles. Other requirements for playing are listed in this column. In addition, some games appear to be very silly, and sometimes participants would rather not have others watch. These are also noted in this column. Almost all the games can be done indoors or out. Where this is not the case, it is indicated.

• **Appropriate social purposes** gives you an idea about what games are especially useful for particular social goals. What is suitable for a group of adults may not be appropriate for children and vice versa, so both are indicated as needed. Again, [C] is for children and [A] is for adults.

Openers are nonthreatening and advisable as a first game when presenting New Games.

Icebreakers are good to do near the beginning of a play session and include a lot of overlap with openers. They also include games that are slightly riskier (that is, they involve touching or seeming silly) than any of the openers and create further good feelings among players.

Getting acquainted games involve a bit more psychological risk than those in the previous categories and should be introduced after a playful mood has been established with players so that they are ready and willing to take more of a chance.

Preliminary trust building games are good for taking a group a stage further in bonding and trust; they can also be used before the trust activities outlined in chapter 7.

Team building games are activities that help create a positive feeling of togetherness and cohesiveness.

Bringing closure games bring the group together in order to end a session. There is a lot of overlap between closing games for adults and children, but, for the sake of clarity, these are listed separately.

• **Skills needed and developed** will be particularly useful for teachers. Although the main point of New Games is not just to get exercise or to teach social skills (in case you forgot, the games are primarily for fun and for including everyone who wants to join), they inherently include many developmental skills. The skills, based on Gerhard Hecker's book *Kompendium Didaktik Sport*, are listed here with definitions for those that could be ambiguous:

Cooperation: Working together for a common goal

Problem solving: Finding one out of many possible solutions

Verbal contact: Interaction with speech (includes listening skills)

Tactile contact: Physical touching

Adaptability: Responsiveness to fit the actions and movements of others

Self-control: Ability to direct the body, speech, and mind

Creativity: Using ideas inventively

Spontaneity: Impromptu action without special instructions given

Pantomime: Expression through acting movements

Visual ability: Observation and peripheral perception

Skillfulness and coordination: Complex body movements

Reaction: Quick physical response

Speed: Quickness in running

Strength

Endurance

Running

Throwing and catching

Jumping

Balance

Climbing

Leaning on

Crawling

Before you get to the game finder, here are two lists of games that did not fit there. The first list, games that support curriculum, should be quite useful to teachers; the second list, games that include singing, is just useful, period.

• **Games that support curriculum.** All of the games require listening, concentrating, and following instructions. Most of the games with an activity level higher than low are good for physical education. Here are some other skills and corresponding games that support the curriculum:

Simple math: Bloomps

Left–right distinction: Bumpity, Bump, Bump, Bump; Ship Ahoy; Line Up; Captain Video; Elephant, Rabbit, Palm Tree; People to People; Zoom

Language: Cranes and Crows, In the Manner of the Adverb, Little Ernie, Three-Syllable Game, Scoot and Spell, A Day At The Races, Ain't No Flies On Us, A What?, Bear Hunt, Bloomps, I Have A Friend . . . , I Sit in the Grass With My Friend . . . , La Ba Doo, Lemonade, Mnemonic Names, People to People, Say Something Nice, Ship Ahoy!, Sun Monarch, This Is My Nose, Um-Ah

Memory: Bumpity, Bump, Bump, Bump; I Sit in the Grass With My Friend . . . ; The Last Detail; Mnemonic Names; Ship Ahoy!; Captain Video; Group Juggle; This Is My Nose; Line Up; A What?; Little Ernie; Robots; Scoot and Spell; Sun Monarch; Zip, Zap, Pop; Zoom

Listening skills: Four Corners; This Is My Nose; Three-Syllable Game; Bloomps; Cows and Ducks; Huddle Up; I Have a Friend . . . ; I Sit in the Grass With My Friend . . . ; Little Ernie; Mnemonic Names; Musical Chairs Unlimited; Name Echo; Partner Game; People to People; Rain Game; Pruie; Robots; Sardines; Ship Ahoy!; Sun Monarch; Zip, Zap, Pop; Aura; Greeting Game, and the explanations for every game

Attention to detail: The Last Detail; Pruie; This Is My Nose; A Day At The Races; A What?; Bloomps; Bumpity, Bump, Bump, Bump; Captain

Video; Cranes and Crows; Elephant, Rabbit, Palm Tree; Group Juggle; Face Pass; Knights, Mounts, Cavaliers; Lemonade; Line Up; Little Ernie; Mnemonic Names; Monarch; Name Echo; Partner Game; People to People; Rain Game; Scoot and Spell; Ship Ahoy!; Sleeper; Sleeping Lions; Three-Syllable Game; Wink; Zip, Zap, Pop; Zoom; Blind Run; Greeting Game

Simple anatomy: People to People, This Is My Nose, La Ba Doo, Face Pass

Social skills: Say Something Nice, I Have a Friend . . . , Ain't No Flies On Us, A What?, Base Tag, Borrow It, Car-Car, Car Wash, Cat and Mice, Elbow Tag, Energy, Huddle Up, Hug Tag, Human Spring, Knots and Giant Knot, La Ba Doo, Lap Game, Loose Caboose, Monarch, Octopus, Partner Tag, People to People, Pruie, Quack, Robots, Sardines, Scoot and Spell, Spiral, Ultimate Foam Ball, Blind Run, Body Surfing, Greeting Game, Trust Leap, Trust Lift, Willow in the Wind

Any subject: Sun Monarch

- **Games that use a song.** Songs are good for focusing the attention of the group and drawing in members. The songs presented here are lighthearted and funny. In most situations, they can help alleviate tension and create a good feeling among players. Occasionally, they may not be appropriate, such as if a tragedy has recently occurred. The first two and perhaps the last one are more for children—although not only, while La Ba Doo could be used with adults, even in a business setting.

A Rum Sum Sum

Bear Hunt

La Ba Doo

Um-Ah

The activity level of each game is clear from the chapter title located in the lower right corner of the right-side page.

The game finder follows. When combined with the information in chapter 1, it should enable you to plan play sessions that include everyone for a whopping good time!

Game Finder

LOW, LOW/MODERATE, MODERATE, AND HIGH ACTIVITY GAMES					
Name of game	Page number	Activity level	When to play	Number of players	
A Day at the Races	80	Low/moderate	Any time	5-50+	
Ain't No Flies on Us	40	Low	Middle	5-50+	
Amoeba	82	Low/moderate	Middle End	5-50+	
A Rum Sum Sum	84	Low/moderate	Any time [C] Middle [A]	5-50+	
A What?	38	Low	Middle	10-20	
Base Tag	162	High	Any time	10-50+	
Bear Hunt	86	Low/moderate	Any time [C] Middle [A] End [A]	5-50+	
Blob	164	High	Any time	10-50+	
Bloomps	42	Low	Any time	10-35	
Borrow It	166	High	Any time	10-50+	
Bumpity, Bump, Bump, Bump	44	Low	Middle	5-35	
Captain Video	46	Low	Middle	5-10	
Car-Car	122	Moderate	Middle	6-50+	
Car Wash	124	Moderate	Middle End	5-35	
Cat and Mice	168	High	Middle End	10-50	
Caterpillar	126	Moderate	Middle End	5-35	
Choo Choo	128	Moderate	Beginning Middle	10-50+	
Clothespin Tag	170	High	Any time	5-50+	

	Special space and equipment needed	Appropriate social purposes	Primary skills needed or developed
	Soft surface	Bringing closure [C]	Tactile contact, pantomime, balance
	Enough room for 2 lines of players to take 3 steps each	Team building, bringing closure [C]	Verbal contact, adaptability
	Enough room for groups of players to have a short race (minimum 20 feet)	Preliminary trust building, team building, bringing closure	Cooperation, problem solving, verbal and tactile contact, self-control
		Opener [C], bringing closure [A&C]	Skillfulness and coordination
	Enough room for a close circle of players; objects to pass	Getting acquainted	Self-control, verbal contact, adaptability, problem solving
	Enough room to allow movement; 1 ball per 5 players; 1 base per 3 players	Icebreaker	Throwing and catching, running, speed, visual ability
		Opener [C], bringing closure [A&C]	Skillfulness and coordination, verbal contact, adaptability
	Large space [C]; boundary markers if possible	Bringing closure	Running, cooperation, verbal and tactile contact, reaction, self-control, visual ability, speed
	Enough room for a circle of players; chairs, if older players	Bringing closure [C]	Verbal contact, multiplication
	Minimum 20 by 20 feet; hula hoops or other bases; 4 or 5 objects for each team	Opener [C], bringing closure [C]	Running, self-control, adaptability, visual ability
		Getting acquainted	Reaction, self-control
		Getting acquainted	Pantomime, visual ability
	Space large enough to allow some movement	Preliminary trust building, team building	Visual ability, balance, self-control
	Room for two lines of players; soft surface if possible	Preliminary trust building, team building, bringing closure	Tactile contact, crawling, leaning on, self-control, creativity
	Large area on a soft surface, if possible; boundary markers	Preliminary trust building, team building, bringing closure [A&C]	Tactile contact, adaptability, running, strength, cooperation, self-control
	Room for at least 1 line of players; soft surface: mats, grass, or carpet	Preliminary trust building, team building, bringing closure	Tactile contact, self-control
	Maybe a secluded space	Getting acquainted, team building	Verbal contact
	Minimum 20 square feet to allow movement; clothespins	Opener, bringing closure [C]	Adaptability, tactile contact, self-control, visual ability, skillfulness and coordination, reaction, running, speed

(continued) ⟹

Game Finder *(continued)*

Special space and equipment needed	Appropriate social purposes	Primary skills needed or developed
Space for players to move around; no obstacles	Preliminary trust building, team building	Tactile contact, adaptability, self-control, trust
Large, open space; boundary markers	Icebreaker, team building	Adaptability, running, tactile contact, reaction
Unobstructed area large enough to allow chasing	Preliminary trust building	Reaction, adaptability, speed, tactile contact, self-control, visual ability
	Icebreaker, team building	Reaction, pantomime
	Opener [A], icebreaker [C], preliminary trust building	Tactile contact, self-control, reaction
Large space in gym or outdoors; large soft foam ball, bat; 1 base	Icebreaker, team building, bringing closure [C]	Throwing and catching, running, cooperation, speed, self-control, reaction
Minimum 30 by 30 feet; boundary markers	Opener, preliminary trust building	Running, speed, self-control, visual ability, reaction
Room for close circle of players	Getting acquainted, bringing closure	Creativity, spontaneity, pantomime, adaptability, visual ability
Gym, large activity room, or outdoors	Icebreaker, team building, game to finish [C]	Running, jumping, speed
Room for players to move in a square	Opener [C], bringing closure [C]	Self-control
Large space; if smaller space, slow game down; boundary markers	Icebreaker	Running, reaction, tactile contact, speed, visual ability, adaptability
Room for large circle of players; 3-5 foam balls	Team building	Throwing and catching, adaptability, self-control, visual ability, cooperation, skillfulness and coordination
Room for the group to mingle about	Preliminary trust building, team building	Tactile contact, creativity, reaction
Minimum 30 square feet; 3-5 foam balls or other objects	Sensitivity and trust game, team building, bringing closure [A]	Reaction, running, speed, endurance
Soft surface: carpeting, mats, or grass	Preliminary trust game	Cooperation, leaning on, trust, verbal contact, self-control, strength
Place markers or chairs; plenty of room	Opener, team building, bringing closure	Tactile contact, self-control, visual ability, speed
Place markers or chairs	Opener [C]	Self-control, reaction
Room for players to act out adverbs; should be somewhat clear of obstacles	Bringing closure [C]	Problem solving, self-control, creativity, pantomime, visual ability
Room for players to move around; music player or singer	Icebreaker, getting acquainted	Self-control, reaction, adaptability, visual ability

(continued) ➠

Game Finder *(continued)*

Special space and equipment needed	Appropriate social purposes	Primary skills needed or developed
	Opener [A], icebreaker [C], preliminary trust building, team building, bringing closure	Problem solving, tactile contact, cooperation, skillfulness and coordination
Room for large circle of players	Getting acquainted, team building, bringing closure	Tactile contact, self-control
Soft surface	Preliminary trust building, team building, bringing closure	Cooperation, self-control, balance
Enough space to fit players; clothes are equipment	Icebreaker	Visual ability, problem solving
30-foot-wide space clear of obstacles; boundary markers	Icebreaker, bringing closure	Creativity, pantomime, visual ability, reaction, problem solving, speed, running, self-control
Unobstructed space for a square of players	Opener [A], team building, bringing closure [A]	Reaction, running, visual ability, self-control, cooperation
Large, clear area to hold lines of players	Icebreaker	Self-control, reaction
Space for two circles	Getting acquainted, bringing closure [A&C]	Reaction, visual ability
Large, clear space 30 by 30 feet; boundary markers	Icebreaker, team building, bringing closure	Tactile contact, running, cooperation, reaction, self-control
	Getting acquainted, team building	Verbal contact, self-control
Minimum 30 by 30 feet; foam ball and boundary markers	Team building, bringing closure [A&C]	Throwing and catching, reaction, cooperation, running, visual ability, verbal contact, adaptability, self-control, endurance
Indoors is best but can be done outdoors; chairs or markers and music player	Team building, bringing closure	Tactile contact, self-control, reaction, balance
Enough room for large circle of players	Icebreaker, team building	Creativity, spontaneity
Minimum 30 by 30 feet; 1 or 2 foam balls and boundary markers	Opener [C]	Running, adaptability, visual ability, speed, pantomime, reaction
Enough room for players to move in their own space	Opener [C]	Adaptability, cooperation, self-control, visual ability
Room for group to stand and move about	Getting acquainted	Cooperation, visual ability, reaction
Minimum 10 by 10 feet open space; larger if more than 10 people	Icebreaker	Adaptability, spontaneity, reaction, visual ability, self-control
Minimum 30 by 30 feet	Getting acquainted, bringing closure [A]	Tactile contact, cooperation, self-control, speed
Unobstructed open space 15 square feet minimum; out of public view	Bringing closure [A], preliminary trust building, getting acquainted, team building	Tactile contact

(continued) ➡

Game Finder *(continued)*

Name of game	Page number	Activity level	When to play	Number of players	
LOW, LOW/MODERATE, MODERATE, AND HIGH ACTIVITY GAMES					
Quack!	106	Low/moderate	Middle End	2-35	
Rain Game	108	Low/moderate	Any time	5-50+	
Robots	110	Low/moderate	Middle	5-50+	
Rotation Baseball	190	High	Middle	4-50+	
Sardines	112	Low/moderate	Middle, best at night if indoors	5-20	
Say Something Nice	114	Low/moderate	Any time	5-35	
Scoot and Spell	154	Moderate	Middle	10-35	
Serve It Up	192	High	Beginning	5-50	
Ship Ahoy!	156	Moderate	Any time	5-50+	
Sleeper	116	Low/moderate	Middle	10-35	
Sleeping Lions	64	Low	Middle End [A]	10-35	
Snowball	158	Moderate	Beginning Middle	5-50+	
Spiral	118	Low/moderate	Middle End	10-35	
Sun Monarch	66	Low	Any time	10-35	
This Is My Nose	68	Low	Middle [A] End [A&C]	5-35	
Three-Syllable Game	70	Low	Middle	5-50+	
Ultimate Foam Ball	194	High	Middle End	5-35	
Um-Ah	72	Low	Middle End [A]	2-50+	

Special space and equipment needed	Appropriate social purposes	Primary skills needed or developed
Enough space for group to move a little; might want secluded space	Getting acquainted, preliminary trust building [A]	Balance, tactile contact
	Opener, team building, bringing closure [A&C]	Self-control, cooperation, skillfulness and coordination
Enough room for players to move around	Icebreaker, team building, preliminary trust building	Verbal contact, tactile contact
Large space: gym or outdoors; bat, ball, 2 bases for every 4 or 5 players	Team building	Skillfulness and coordination, running, throwing, catching, visual ability, self-control, speed, cooperation
Big place with many large hiding places	Getting acquainted, team building	Problem solving, visual ability, tactile contact, cooperation
Foam ball	Getting acquainted, team building, bringing closure	Verbal contact, visual ability, throwing and catching, cooperation
20 by 20 feet minimum; 150 small index cards	Team building	Problem solving, cooperation, verbal contact, self-control, creativity, spontaneity, running
Room to allow players free movement (30 by 30 feet); many objects; object holder	Opener	Self-control, visual ability, spontaneity, skillfulness and coordination, running, speed
Room to allow players free movement; cones or other markers (optional)	Icebreaker	Self-control, reaction, problem solving, speed, pantomime
Enough space for players to mingle	Icebreaker	Problem solving, visual ability, pantomime
Enough space for group to mingle	Getting acquainted, bringing closure [A]	Self-control, creativity, problem solving
Minimum 20 by 20 feet; paper, pen and pencil; boundaries	Opener [A]	Throwing, adaptability, self-control, visual ability, skillfulness and coordination, catching, reaction
	Getting acquainted, team building, bringing closure [A]	Tactile contact, self-control, cooperation
Enough room for group to move from one side to the other; one place marker	Getting acquainted, bringing closure [C]	Creativity, problem solving, verbal contact
	Bringing closure [C]	Problem solving, verbal contact, adaptability
Enough room for players to divide into 3 groups 10 feet apart	Team building	Problem solving, cooperation, verbal contact, creativity
Large space, 50 by 30 feet minimum; foam ball and boundary markers	Team building, bringing closure	Cooperation, verbal contact, adaptability, self-control, throwing and catching, reaction, running
	Getting acquainted, bringing closure [A]	Pantomime

(continued) ➡

Game Finder *(continued)*

LOW, LOW/MODERATE, MODERATE, AND HIGH ACTIVITY GAMES

Name of game	Page number	Activity level	When to play	Number of players	
Wink	196	High	Middle End	10-35	
Zip, Zap, Pop	74	Low	Middle End [A]	5-20	
Zoom	76	Low	Any time	5-35	

TRUST ACTIVITIES

Name of game	Page number	Activity level	When to play	Number of players	
Aura	202	Low	Middle	2-50+	
Blind Run	204	Moderate	End	9-21	
Body Surfing	206	Moderate	End	10-50+	
Greeting Game	208	Low/moderate	End	5-50	
Trust Leap	210	High	End	9-20	
Trust Lift	212	High	End	10-20	
Willow in the Wind	214	Moderate	End	7-50	

	Special space and equipment needed	Appropriate social purposes	Primary skills needed or developed
	Soft surface: mats, carpet, grass	Preliminary trust building, bringing closure [C]	Tactile contact, reaction, self-control, crawling, visual ability, strength, leaning on
		Getting acquainted, bringing closure [A]	Reaction, self-control
		Opener [A&C], bringing closure [C]	Self-control

	Space and equipment needed	Appropriate social purposes	Skills needed or developed
	Quiet space with room for pairs to turn around	Trust game	Cooperation, self-control, balance
	Large room with space for two lines to spread out, or open space outside	Trust game	Balance, skillfulness and coordination, cooperation
	Room for a line of players to roll on; soft surface helpful	Trust game	Cooperation, trust, tactile contact, self-control, leaning on
	Soft surface desirable; out of public view is very desirable	Trust game	Spontaneity, crawling, creativity, adaptability, problem solving
	Soft surface; enough room to run and leap into the line	Trust game, team building	Tactile contact, self-control, cooperation, strength, visual ability
	Space to lift a person overhead; soft surface desirable	Trust game, team building	Strength, cooperation, tactile contact
	Soft surface desirable; open space for large group	Trust game, team building	Tactile contact, cooperation, strength, self-control, leaning on, verbal contact, adaptability

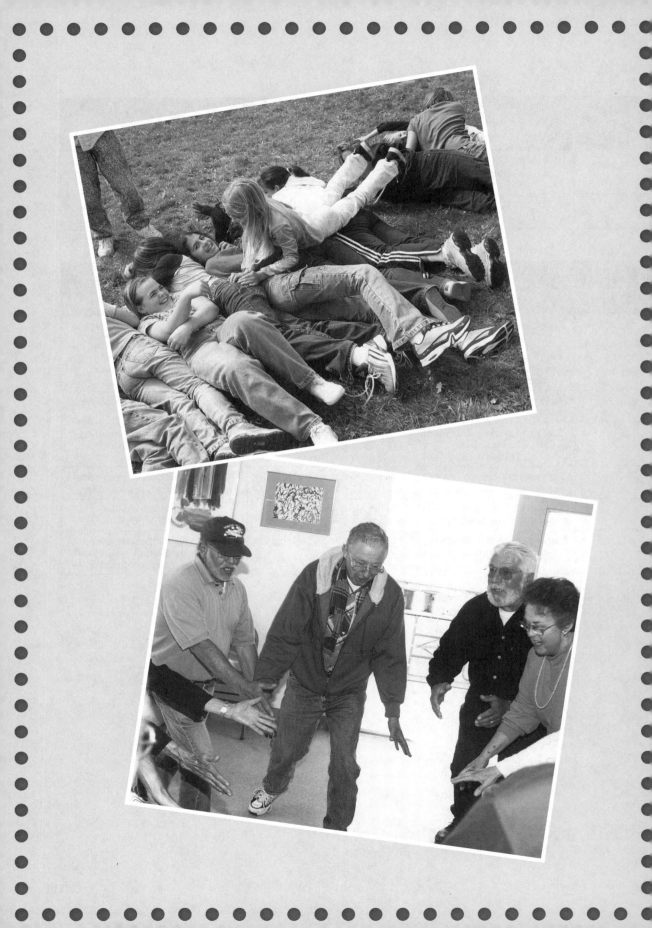

Chapter 1

Using New Games

Opportunities are often things you haven't noticed the first time around.

    —*Catherine Deneuve*

New Games may be thought of by some as a bit of fluff, a respite from the grind of everyday living. I would not deny they are the latter, but I have seen that they are much more than the former.

In the 1990s, animosities among Croats, Serbs, and Muslims in the former Yugoslavia had reached genocidal proportions. The killing had been so widespread and horrific, it was impossible to imagine that these people could come together again under any circumstances. Yet right after the 1993 cease-fire, I found myself teaching New Games to a group of 500 Croats, Serbs, and Muslims at a peace conference in Osijek, Croatia.

Amazingly, the games broke down barriers that talking had not even begun to touch. While the effects of being together and focusing on peace were significant, to actually laugh and have fun together was a powerful healing experience. Nobody seemed to care who was who. The highlight was having uniformed Croatian Army members join us without so much as a flinch from the Serb and Muslim participants.

This experience may sound like a miracle. And it was. While New Games may not always have such profound results, the potential is always there for significant breakthroughs, new insights, and better relationships. And whatever else happens, they're always a lot of fun! In this chapter we'll briefly see where New Games came from, and how you can use them to help all kinds of people have a great time together.

The History of New Games

*Of course I want to win it . . . I'm not here to have a good time,
nor to keep warm and dry.*

—*Nick Faldo, golfer*

To see where New Games began, we need to go back to the Vietnam War era. Stewart Brand, who edited the *Whole Earth Catalog*, was looking for ways for people to express their aggression without hurting each other. One result was an event at San Francisco State University called "World War IV," which featured a form of conflict called "Soft War" games. (At that time, it looked like World War III, if it happened, could be a nuclear war, so Stewart decided to skip WW III and go on to WW IV!) These games are very physical, but safe.

Soft War games are played in a confined area so that anyone outside the boundaries is not touched. Any time a player decides the game is too much, he or she can simply step outside the borders and be out of the game. The surface that the games are played on is soft—whether it is grass, sand, or gym mats—significantly reducing the likelihood of injuries. However, the most important safety feature of Soft War games is the agreement at the beginning of every game that if anyone yells or says "Stop," all players agree to do so. In this way, people can self-referee and keep themselves from getting hurt.

Stewart was not interested in discouraging competition because he felt that people who were opposed to warfare in any form, including competitive games, were also very out of touch with their bodies in an unhealthy way. Soft War was a way to encourage people to become more aware of their bodies and to channel their competitive, aggressive selves in a creative, powerful, fun, and safe way. The New Games motto, "Play Hard, Play Fair, Nobody Hurt," originated with this in mind.

The next big event was the first New Games tournament, where people were invited to come and share their games. Not long after this, Stewart's attention moved on to other areas. But a group of people, including forward-looking recreation and parks professionals, thought the New Games idea was a positive phenomenon that ought to be encouraged. So they incorporated the nonprofit educational New Games Foundation in 1974. The foundation lasted for 10 years and refined the concept of New Games, spreading the movement through hundreds of training workshops in North America and beyond.

What evolved was a blend of elements from the human potential and creative play movements. The human potential movement contributed ideas such as trust games, where a person had to trust fellow players to take care of him or her; and creative play brought in the idea that the players could create the game and then change it to make it work better for them.

The reason for the ongoing popularity of New Games is that, unlike most sports or recreational activities, they can be played and enjoyed by anyone.

While this includes people of different ages like parents, grandparents, and children, it goes far beyond that. The games can be adapted for people with many different physical and mental abilities. New Games have been played with prisoners, people of all socioeconomic groups, people of different racial and ethnic backgrounds, people of both sexes, and members of different religions. The most remarkable fact is that people from all these groups are often playing the games together.

The uses of New Games keep expanding. Teachers use them to present lessons or teach physical and personal skills (see pages xxiv-xxxiii for a list of skills developed). Businesses use the games to improve communication, for team building, and for conflict resolution. Almost every group has used the games as ice breakers. While not a cure-all, the New Games idea has proven useful in a wide variety of situations such as mental health and physical rehabilitation. For this reason, New Games will continue to exist and flourish. One need not be a spectator in a world increasingly given over to experts and specialists. With New Games, everyone who chooses to play can do so.

Leading New Games

> *We always admire the other fellow more after we have tried to do his job.*
>
> —*William Feather*

However New Games are presented, people usually enjoy them. If the group is the least bit interested, people will get caught up in the spirit of the games. But if you pay attention to the suggestions in this chapter, play will go even better.

Be Safety Conscious

The most important and often most overlooked aspect of leading any game is to make sure that it is safe. The leader must be aware of both the physical and psychological safety of players.

Physical Safety

Before a session begins, indoors or out, a leader must examine the play area for potential dangers (such as poles, holes, sharp edges, obstacles, wet spots, and animal droppings) that need to be noted or removed. Be sure to inform players about anything they should be aware of before starting a specific game.

The way the games are introduced will help determine how players will interact. By being playful, humorous, and responsive to comments from participants, the leader can establish a playful and relaxed mood to play the games.

For active games, make sure players remember that the idea is to have fun and not play so hard that they hurt others. When a game gets too rough, you can stop it and either change to another game or change the rules to make it safer. Asking the group how to change the game to keep it safe gives the group ownership of the game. But remember to make only one change at a time. More than that may confuse your players.

When it looks as if a player is hurt, move the group away and make sure someone looks after the person. Usually, the problem is minor and the player just needs a private moment to recover. If the person is truly hurt, which is rarely the case, see to it that he or she gets the necessary help. Make sure to carry a cell (mobile) phone or ask someone to make a call to emergency services. (Didn't mean to scare you! In all honesty, this has never happened at my sessions.)

Psychological Safety

As a games leader, you have a responsibility to create an atmosphere where everyone feels safe. There are many ways of doing this; one way is for a leader to participate in the games. This gives the players confidence, increasing their psychological safety. It shows that you are not trying to get them to do something that you would not do or to pull some kind of trick on them. You do not have to play every minute of every game, but be willing to at least demonstrate a game. Be the first to go into a game that people might think is a bit foolish or risky. If the leader is willing to play the fool, it makes it easier for players to do so.

Also, it is okay for a few of the players to decide to sit a game out, or "pass." If a person is genuinely frightened, he needs to be able to choose not to play. However, if someone is just trying to be cool (as might be the case with adolescents), I suggest coaxing him to join with "Come on, just try this!" You have to make a judgment call about what a person is doing. In games like Face Pass and Name Echo, where participants are called on to be creative, allow a person to say "pass" if she is stuck or feels too shy. Having choice is important. Remember, these games often look silly and take many players out of their comfort zone. If you get the group to go along and take risks, it becomes easier and safer for an individual to take a risk, too. In this way, you give permission to people to do things they might not ordinarily do. Most often, they come around.

Once when I was in Stockholm, Sweden, presenting New Games in a small city park, I noticed an older gentleman watching us intently from across the street. I yelled over to him, "You're welcome to join us!" He shook his head "no." I went on presenting games and the next time I was aware of him, he was on our side of the street, still looking quite interested. Again I invited him, and again he declined. When I saw him next, he had joined us! Later he told me, "When you invited me, each time I thought, *I'm too old.* Finally I thought, *I'm not too old.*"

Demonstrate

Many people are visual learners, and demonstrating gives them a useful visual image to accompany your explanation. For clarity, arrange the players in the formation they need to be in to start the game (for example, in a circle, a line, or with a partner) before you begin the demonstration. Then you can walk them through the game in the physical context in which they will be playing. This allows players to practice the game so they will understand it better before playing. A verbal explanation alone leaves visual learners adrift. Again, when a game looks a little risky, be the first to participate.

Varying Your Presentation

How you present the game will vary with the makeup of your group. For young players, you might use a fairy tale–like story to introduce a game, but this approach would not usually be appropriate for teens or business groups.

For example, the game of Energy has the group holding hands in a circle. The energy is passed from person to person with a gentle hand squeeze. With a group of children, I might say, "Imagine you are the ocean, and a wave comes by. You can tell the wave is passing because your neighbor will squeeze your hand gently and lift it up. You will then do the same to your neighbor on the other side. Let's watch the wave go across the water." This gives the kids an image they can understand and a movement to go with it that catches their attention; this helps to keep them focused.

With a business group, I might introduce the same game like this: "We are experiencing an energy crisis, and the only way to get electricity to everyone is to relay it from person to person with a hand squeeze." The emphasis with both groups is on acting as a team, but the presentation is different.

Maintain a Playful and Inviting Attitude

A games leader who never smiles or laughs will have a hard time convincing others to relax and have fun. By having fun yourself, you will provide encouragement for others to do the same. A key to making the games work is your enthusiasm and enjoyment of what you are doing. So pick games and activities that you like. Your joy will be infectious. Whenever you see curious spectators, invite them to join. Although you should never try to force someone to participate, people appreciate knowing they are welcome if they decide to join. Likewise, if someone says she has a game she would like to share, be open to trying it. The main times to step in are if some aspect of the game is not safe, or if the game is not working. In both cases, you can either make suggestions or invite the players to brainstorm on making the game safer or more fun.

Keeping the Group's Attention

It helps to know a variety of games so that you can move freely from active to passive (more restful) games. Watch the attention level of the group closely, and switch activities if they are getting too exhausted to pay attention or too bored to do so. Without the group's attention, the energy will dissipate and the games will not go as well. With kids, it is useful to learn some techniques for getting attention, such as doing a rhythmic clap that the group must duplicate (the noise alone alerts them) or saying, "Everyone who can hear me raise an arm." Another way to keep interest up is to make use of whatever dramatic flair you can muster. One time when I was in Israel, I raised my voice and said, "Let's start the games." No one seemed to notice; they just kept talking to one another. In a very loud voice, I boomed, "Okay, it's time to start." No response. I knew I had to capture their attention, but I did not know how to do it. At this point, I spontaneously started throwing my arms and legs about while making strange whoops and yells. They thought I had gone crazy, so they stopped talking and looked at me. As soon as I noticed their change, I promptly stopped and calmly said, "Let's do some New Games." Note that you can do a specific thing like that only once with the same group.

When presenting New Games with a group that does not understand your language well, slow down while speaking, simplify your explanation, enunciate your words, and spend more time demonstrating the game to make it clear. If many people do not know your language at all, have someone translate. You should stop every sentence or two so that the translator can do a proper job and allow participants to follow along. It is useful if someone translates back to you any discussion, comments, or questions so that you can stay with the discussion. In one workshop I did in South Africa in a center for people with cognitive disabilities, I presented Zoom, where the sound "zoom" is passed from person to person around the circle. At some point, the players changed the zoom to an Afrikaans word, *soen,* and started laughing. I felt left out, so I asked what it meant; I was told by a giddy player, "Kiss!"

Adapting Games

Education is when you read the fine print. Experience is what you get when you don't.

—Pete Seeger

Any game can be done with almost any group. However, it may not always look quite the same, because a game may need to be changed either a little or a lot. How we do the game with active people in their early 20s is not how we would do it with elderly or preschool players or players with disabilities. When presenting a game, you need to take into account the capabilities of the group, the appropriateness of the game for that group, and their mood at the moment, and you need to make changes accordingly. Here are some suggested changes:

- Avoid embarrassment for a single person having to guess by having more than one person guessing.
- Have players who are reluctant to hold hands hold on to a sleeve or short piece of cloth or string, at least to start with.
- Take restless kids from a small play area to a large one for an active game.
- Slow down an active game for a group of elderly people.
- Use fairy tale–like stories to introduce games and to interest preschool children.
- Restrict boundaries for an active game with tired or elderly players.
- Find ways to include players who are left over when partners are required, such as using three instead of two.
- Use games that will help people mix in when they don't know one another.
- Have an older person hold hands with a very young child who is frightened.
- Handicap any able players when including players with physical disabilities (though this is not always necessary—players with disabilities may self-adapt).
- Include people who choose not to play by having them set up boundaries or look after players whose eyes are closed to make sure the players do not run into anything or anyone.

Of course, these suggestions do not cover every situation you will find yourself in when presenting the games, but they will give you an idea of how to approach unexpected challenges. Thinking things up on your own is part of the fun because it stimulates your imagination and calls on your creativity.

On the other hand, who said you were on your own? Taking suggestions from players is stimulating for them, and implementing their ideas gives them ownership of the game. The game changes from "your" game to "our" game. Making this change is subtle, but it's important. When people feel their imagination is engaged, they also feel responsibility for the game. The game stands a better chance of succeeding, especially if you have miscalculated something about the group. If, for example, you have underestimated the capabilities of the group when making adaptations, that will not matter if you welcome the input of the players, as we see in Saved by the Players (see page 8).

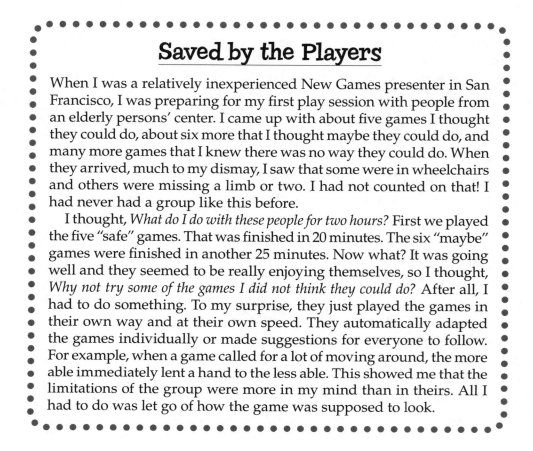

Saved by the Players

When I was a relatively inexperienced New Games presenter in San Francisco, I was preparing for my first play session with people from an elderly persons' center. I came up with about five games I thought they could do, about six more that I thought maybe they could do, and many more games that I knew there was no way they could do. When they arrived, much to my dismay, I saw that some were in wheelchairs and others were missing a limb or two. I had not counted on that! I had never had a group like this before.

I thought, *What do I do with these people for two hours?* First we played the five "safe" games. That was finished in 20 minutes. The six "maybe" games were finished in another 25 minutes. Now what? It was going well and they seemed to be really enjoying themselves, so I thought, *Why not try some of the games I did not think they could do?* After all, I had to do something. To my surprise, they just played the games in their own way and at their own speed. They automatically adapted the games individually or made suggestions for everyone to follow. For example, when a game called for a lot of moving around, the more able immediately lent a hand to the less able. This showed me that the limitations of the group were more in my mind than in theirs. All I had to do was let go of how the game was supposed to look.

Creating Games

If you want creative workers, give them enough time to play.

—*John Cleese*

In one sense, it is almost impossible to invent an entirely new New Game. When I found or made up a New Game and shared it with groups during my travels, almost invariably somebody would say, "Oh, that's such-and-such," or "That's not new. I played something like that when I was a child."

While I was working with the New Games Foundation in San Francisco, the staff figured that there were only about 10 basic games in the world (e.g., tag, hide and seek, throw and catch) and infinite variations and combinations of those. In any case, we never made a claim that New Games were actually new, but rather that the attitude with which we played them was; compared to the prevailing emphasis on winning competitive games, our attitude of playing for fun and including everyone seemed new. Mostly we were able to create games that were new in our experience. As players, we were used to organized games such as basketball and volleyball. No one had ever played games like Pruie or Quack! before. Can you create games, too? Absolutely!

Go With the Flow

Sometimes creating games happens spontaneously. Once, for example, a colleague, Jeff McKay, and I were giving games sessions at a school in San Leandro, California. One day we were with a class of kids who had a lot of anger and anxiety and who were out of control. Fight after fight broke out over nothing: The tension of the fast-approaching Christmas holiday was apparently too much for them. Their homes were often not joyous places to be, and the extended holiday brought so much dread that they did not know what to do with themselves. It was all we could do to cool them down.

Finally, when our time together was ending, I picked up my meter-high oblong equipment bag, filled it, and started to leave. As I did, one of the kids gave it a kick. Instead of scolding him, I reacted by immediately lifting it off the ground and saying, "Have another kick," which the boy immediately did. You could see by the way he beamed with pleasure that he really enjoyed venting his anger and anxiety. The other boys were watching, and, as soon as they saw it was okay with me, they wanted a turn, too. As the would-be Bruce Lees administered their best "death" blows to my equipment bag, they all got happy faces.

At last I told them I had to leave to go to another class. Without hesitation, one of the boys volunteered to hold the bag in my absence, promising to return it when they were done. In essence, these young fellows created a "soft war" game and took over responsibility for maintaining it. I had learned a valuable lesson: All I had to do was go with their energy instead of against it for their creativity to burst forth.

Use a Grid

Here is a technique for creating a game from nothing with a group of people. This might seem complicated at first, but it is actually quite simple. It's great fun and worth learning as an activity to stimulate players' imaginations. First, make a large grid on a board or flip chart like the grid on page 10. Then write the numbers 0 to 9 randomly down the left side so you end up with two numbers in each box. Next, write three elements of a game across the top. Then take suggestions to fill the grid. At one workshop where I used this device, the players came up with the grid on page 10.

Once we had our grid, I divided the group into subgroups of five or six people and asked each group to pick a number between 100 and 999. We matched up the first digit with the line in the first column that was preceded by that digit. In this way, it was determined which item from that column would be an element in the game. Likewise, the second digit was matched

	Type of players	Action or movement	Fantasy
0 and 1	Acting like 10-year-olds	Running	Caterpillars
2 and 5	Acting like elderly people	Movement changes	On the moon
4 and 6	Blind or with closed eyes	Crabwalk	Monkeys
7 and 9	Switching roles	Jumping a narrow corridor	Passing along
3 and 8	Having eye contact	Crawling	Underwater

with the line in the second column preceded by that digit; whatever line the third digit matched, of course, determined which item was picked from the third column.

For example, one group at the workshop picked the number 894. If you look at the grid, you can see the 8 in the row with "Having eye contact" in the "Type of players" column. The second digit, 9, corresponds with "Jumping" in the second column. Finally, the third digit, 4, goes with "Monkeys" in the third column, "Fantasy."

So this group had to create a game that involved having eye contact, jumping, and monkeys. We also used objects that we found in addition to whatever normal equipment was available (i.e., foam balls, cones). An example of what we found at this particular workshop: matches, tree branches, stones, and feathers.

Monkey Jumping, Narrow Passage, and Rolling Caterpillars are some games that resulted from this grid.

Monkey Jumping

9 to 15 players, moderate activity.

A tag game called Monkey Jumping was created by the group that picked 894. In this game, players are paired in a circle, except for one player who is in the middle. One of the players in each pair holds a branch, which makes him or her the tree, while the other partner, who stands behind him or her, is the monkey.

Whenever two monkeys make eye contact, they immediately have to "jump" by switching trees. The player in the middle then runs to catch a monkey by tagging him or her before the monkey reaches its new tree. If the catcher is successful, she and the monkey switch roles. If the catcher is unsuccessful, the monkey and tree switch roles after the monkey arrives safely, thus giving everyone a chance to jump. Monkey Jumping was so popular that the other groups creating games joined this one, too.

I used to use a larger grid by giving each number from 0 to 9 a line of its own that we would fill with possibilities. In practice, however, I found that this took too long to do. Keeping the grid simple by using only a few categories for elements and combining numbers randomly (e.g., 1 and 7, 2 and 9) allows us to make a game of filling the grid, tapping the imagination of the participants without the activity becoming tedious.

When you are explaining to the group what kinds of items you need to fill the grid, it helps to provide at least the first example for each column to help make your description clear to the group. This is especially important when they get stuck. It is important that the grid you use be large enough for everyone in the group to see.

Usually, once each group has its elements, they are given 10 minutes (15 at most!) to invent a game. Since this is an experiment, there should be a balance between discussion and testing. Every group should be encouraged to try all ideas rather than intellectualize about what sounds right. The rule is to not criticize someone's suggestion but to just try it. Point out to your players that sometimes the dumbest-sounding ideas turn out to be the most fun!

Narrow Passage

10 to 25 players, moderate activity.

Another group at the Danish workshop came up with the number 727, which called for switching roles (7), changing movements (2), and passing through a corridor (7). The game that evolved from these elements featured a narrow rectangular play area, about 40 feet long by 20 feet wide (12 by 6 meters), with all but two of the players at one of the short ends. Each of the two remaining players stands at the middle of one of the long sides outside of the passage, and both have a soft foam ball. One of the two players tells all the other players how to cross the "narrow passage" (all at the same time) to get to the other side, by, for instance, hopping on one foot or in a crouching position.

Any player hit by one of the balls thrown by the two players in the middle while crossing the narrow passage had to trade places and roles with the one who had hit him or her and continue playing.

Not every created game is a sure-fire hit, but the process of tweaking a game is a valuable technique to learn. It sparks creativity and can reveal a hidden reservoir of imagination. And, in any case, it's fun!

Sleeping Beauty

5 to 25 players, low activity.

Once a group got "10-year-olds," "crawling," and "fairy tale" from their grid. What they came up with was a game called Sleeping Beauty, where one person played Sleeping Beauty, who was waiting for a prince to come and awaken her with a kiss (in this case, a touch). A wicked witch guards Sleeping Beauty, and when the witch catches a prince crawling up to rescue the princess, the person who plays the prince must go back to the starting place. To get to Sleeping Beauty, the prince has to freeze before the witch looks, in order to disguise "his" progress. The princes come from all directions in a circle, about 20 feet (6 meters) from the middle, where Sleeping Beauty is. When a prince reaches Sleeping Beauty, a new Sleeping Beauty and witch are chosen. Many women played princes; however, the funniest part was the two big men playing the witch and Sleeping Beauty!

Taking the Grid a Step Further

Of course, there are many other elements of games that are not mentioned that can either be used as a category in a grid (constructed like the one on page 10) or simply used as suggestions to help groups create a game. For instance, there is a category "defined roles" with elements such as tag with an "it" and "not-its." Other suggestions for roles include hiders and seekers, two teams, partners, liberators, and goal keepers.

Another possibility for a category in the grid is to add rituals, with elements such as a chant or movement to start the game. Or, we could have a category of different forms such as a circle, square, line, or opposing lines. Also, a category of objective could be added with possible elements such as throwing, capturing, fleeing, guessing, freeing, or problem solving. Finally, we could add a category called environment, which could be places such as a closet, corridor, living room, classroom, auditorium, or field.

Chapter 2

Developing Skills and Meeting Standards With New Games

New Games are done for fun and include everyone, but they also encompass a whole range of skills: motor (e.g., running, throwing and catching, skillfulness, and coordination), social (e.g., cooperation and self-control), communication (e.g., verbal and tactile contact), academic (e.g., language and mathematics), and learning (e.g., **listening, concentration,** and **following directions**—these particular learning skills are not indicated with each game in the developmental skills section since they are an integral part of every game in this book). These skills and more apply to established standards from various countries, which are documented in the following tables.

Australia

New South Wales Standards: Stage Outcomes, Table 1

Early stage 1	Stage 1	Stage 2	Stage 3	Stage 4	Stage 5
INTERPERSONAL RELATIONSHIPS				**SELF AND RELATIONSHIPS**	
IRES1.11 Identifies how individuals care for each other.	IRS1.11 Identifies the ways in which they communicate, cooperate, and care for others.	IRS2.11 Describes how relationships with a range of people enhance well-being.	IRS3.11 Describes roles and responsibilities in developing and maintaining positive relationships.	4.1 Describes and analyzes the influences on a sense of self. 4.2 Identifies and selects strategies that enhance their ability to cope and feel supported. 4.3 Describes the qualities of positive relationships and strategies to address the abuse of power.	5.1 Analyzes how they can support their own and others' sense of self. 5.2 Evaluates their capacity to reflect on and respond positively to challenges. 5.3 Analyzes factors that contribute to positive, inclusive, and satisfying relationships.
GAMES AND SPORTS				**MOVEMENT SKILL AND PERFORMANCE**	
GSES1.8 Demonstrates fundamental movement skills while playing with and sharing equipment.	GSS1.8 Performs fundamental movement skills with equipment in minor games.	GSS2.8 Participates and uses equipment in a variety of games and modified sports.	GSS3.8 Applies movement skills in games and sports that require communication, cooperation, decision making, and observation of rules.	4.4 Demonstrates and refines movement skills in a range of contexts and environments. 4.5 Combines the features and elements of movement composition to perform in a range of contexts and environments.	5.4 Adapts, transfers, and improvises movement skills and concepts to improve performance. 5.5 Composes, performs, and appraises movement in a variety of challenging contexts.

Reprinted from Board of Studies, New South Wales 2007.

New South Wales Standards: Stage Outcomes, Table 2

Early stage 1	Stage 1	Stage 2	Stage 3	Stage 4	Stage 5
ACTIVE LIFESTYLE				**LIFELONG PHYSICAL ACTIVITY**	
ALES1.6 Develops a repertoire of physical activities in which they can participate.	ALS1.6 Participates in physical activity, recognizing that it can be both enjoyable and important for health.	ALS2.6 Discusses the relationship between regular physical activity and health.	ALS3.6 Shows how to maintain and improve the quality of an active lifestyle.	4.9 Describes the benefits of a balanced lifestyle and participation in physical activity. 4.10 Explains how personal strengths and abilities contribute to enjoyable and successful participation in physical activity.	5.9 Formulates goals and applies strategies to enhance participation in lifelong physical activity. 5.10 Adopts roles to enhance their own and others' enjoyment of physical activity.
COMMUNICATING					
COES1.1 Expresses feelings, needs, and wants in appropriate ways.	COS1.1 Communicates appropriately in a variety of ways.	COS2.1 Uses a variety of ways to communicate with and within groups.	COS3.1 Communicates confidently in a variety of situations.	4.11 Selects and uses communication skills and strategies clearly and coherently in a range of new and challenging situations.	5.11 Adapts and evaluates communication skills and strategies to justify opinions, ideas, and feelings in increasingly complex situations.
DECISION MAKING					
DMES1.2 Identifies some options available when making simple decisions.	DMS1.2 Recalls past experiences in making decisions.	DMS2.2 Makes decisions as an individual and as a group member.	DMS3.2 Makes informed decisions and accepts responsibility for consequences.	4.12 Assesses risk and social influences and reflects on personal experience to make informed decisions.	5.12 Adapts and applies decision-making processes and justifies their choices in increasingly demanding contexts.

Reprinted from Board of Studies, New South Wales 2007.

New South Wales Standards: Stage Outcomes, Table 3

Early stage 1	Stage 1	Stage 2	Stage 3	Stage 4	Stage 5
INTERACTING					
INES1.3 Relates well to others in work and play situations.	INS1.3 Develops positive relationships with peers and other people.	INS2.3 Makes positive contributions in group activities.	INS3.3 Acts in ways that enhance the contribution of self and others in a range of cooperative situations.	4.13 Demonstrates cooperation and support of others in social, recreational, and other group contexts.	5.13 Adopts roles and responsibilities that enhance group cohesion and the achievement of personal and group objectives.
MOVING					
MOES1.4 Demonstrates a general awareness of how basic movement skills apply in play and other introductory movement experiences.	MOS1.4 Demonstrates maturing performance of basic movement and compositional skills in a variety of predictable situations.	MOS2.4 Displays a focus on quality of movement in applying movement skills to a variety of familiar and new situations.	MOS3.4 Refines and applies movement skills creatively to a variety of challenging situations.	4.14 Engages successfully in a wide range of movement situations that display an understanding of how and why people move.	5.14 Confidently uses movement to satisfy personal needs and interests.
PROBLEM SOLVING AND PLANNING					
PSES1.5 Seeks help as needed when faced with simple problems.	PSS1.5 Draws on past experiences to solve familiar problems.	PSS2.5 Uses a range of problem-solving strategies.	PSS3.5 Suggests, considers, and selects appropriate alternatives when resolving problems.	4.16 Clarifies the source and nature of problems and draws on personal skills and support networks to resolve them. 4.15 Devises, applies, and monitors plans to achieve short-term and long-term goals.	5.16 Predicts potential problems and develops, justifies, and evaluates solutions. 5.15 Devises, justifies, and implements plans that reflect a capacity to prioritize, think creatively, and use resources effectively.

Reprinted from Board of Studies, New South Wales 2007.

New South Wales Stage 6

In stage 6, personal development, health, and physical education life skills, students will do the following:

1. Develop knowledge, understanding, and skills in the management of issues related to personal growth and development.
2. Develop knowledge and understanding in order to make informed decisions concerning health and lifestyle.
3. Develop skills and informed and responsible values and attitudes that enhance the quality of interpersonal relationships.
4. Develop knowledge, understanding, and skills relating to safe living practices.
5. Develop knowledge, understanding, and skills that facilitate participation in a range of leisure activities.
6. Develop the knowledge and skills to engage in a range of outdoor recreational pursuits.

Reprinted from Board of Studies, New South Wales 2007.

Australian Capital Territory (ACT) Essential Learning Achievements (ELA)

Health and Physical Education Standards

ELA 12 takes action to promote health.

ELA 13 is physically skilled and active.

ELA 14 manages self and relationships.

Interdisciplinary

ELA 4 acts with integrity and regard for others.

ELA 5 contributes to group effectiveness.

Reprinted from Australian Capital Territory 2011.

Northern Territory Key Growth Points 1 to 3

Strands and links	Learners demonstrating evidence of key growth point 1	Learners demonstrating evidence of key growth point 2	Learners demonstrating evidence of key growth point 3
Participating in physical activity and movement	**PA KGP1.1** **Movement** Engage in activities in a structured environment using a range of body movements.	**PA KGP2.1** **Movement** Move around a structured environment and perform simple whole-body movements.	**PA KGP3.1** **Movement** Demonstrate simple movement patterns using various parts of the body.
Links Essential In 4, Col 3, Con 3 **Learning areas:** SOSE, technology and design, arts **Perspectives:** literacy, numeracy	**PA KGP1.2** **Games** Coactively participate in a range of appropriate games.	**PA KGP2.2** **Games** Participate in organized activities where equipment is shared.	**PA KGP3.2** **Games** Display confidence and safe practices in sharing equipment and playing games.
	PA KGP1.3 **Fitness** Participate in activities that explore the use of their bodies and senses.	**PA KGP2.3** **Fitness** Participate in a variety of fun activities that encourage cardiorespiratory endurance.	**PA KGP3.3** **Fitness** Identify their feelings during and after activities and games in a range of environments.
	PA KGP1.4 **Participation** Respond to physical activity.	**PA KGP2.4** **Participation** Participate in a range of physical activities.	**PA KGP3.4** **Participation** Discuss ways to ensure all the class is included in games and activities.

Reprinted from Northern Territory Government, Department of Education and Training.

Northern Territory Bands 1 to 3

Strands and links	Learners demonstrating evidence of band 1	Learners demonstrating evidence of band 2	Learners demonstrating evidence of band 3
Participating in physical activity and movement	**PA 1.1** **Movement** Use simple movement sequences individually, in groups, or in teams.	**PA 2.1** **Movement** Demonstrate control in performing sequences of simple movement patterns.	**PA 3.1** **Movement** Safely perform movement sequences incorporating equipment and displaying consistency and control.
Links Essential In 4, Col 3, Con 3 **Learning areas:** SOSE, technology and design, arts **Perspectives:** literacy, numeracy, environmental	**PA 1.2** **Games** Demonstrate basic motor skills in using equipment safely in a variety of play activities and games.	**PA 2.2** **Games** Apply motor skills with equipment in skill activities and minor games using safe and fair practices.	**PA 3.2** **Games** Perform motor skills proficiently and participate fairly and safely in modified games and sports.
	PA 1.3 **Fitness** Compare aspects of both short and continuous periods of exercise on self and others.	**PA 2.3** **Fitness** Actively participate in activities designed to develop aspects of fitness, such as cardiorespiratory endurance, flexibility, and strength.	**PA 3.3** **Fitness** Actively participate in a range of games, activities, and sports that develop aspects of fitness.
	PA 1.4 **Participation** Identify ways of increasing own participation in physical activity.	**PA 2.4** **Participation** Identify and discuss physical activities that family and friends participate in to be physically active.	**PA 3.4** **Participation** Explore influences that affect their own and others' participation in physical activity.

Reprinted from Northern Territory Government, Department of Education and Training.

Northern Territory Bands 4, 5, and Beyond Band 5

Strands and links	Learners demonstrating evidence of band 4	Learners demonstrating evidence of band 5	Learners demonstrating evidence of beyond band 5
Participating in physical activity and movement	**PA 4.1** **Movement** Develop coordinated actions of the body by performing and modifying movement sequences.	**PA 5.1** **Movement** Perform movement skills at a level for confident and competent participation in physical activity.	**PA 5+.1** **Movement** Evaluate the movement performance of others and provide feedback on improving a component of a movement pattern.
Links Essential In 4, Col 3, Con 3 **Learning areas:** SOSE, technology and design, arts **Perspectives:** literacy, numeracy, environmental	**PA 4.2** **Games** Devise and implement strategies and safe practices in games using and adapting a range of complex motor skills.	**PA 5.2** **Games** Demonstrate strategies and tactics in games and sports to optimize performance and display leadership and collaboration skills in group and team situations.	**PA 5+.2** **Games** Critically evaluate the skills and strategies used in a sport; devise and implement a game plan for an individual or a team physical activity.
	PA 4.3 **Fitness** Analyze their own and others' views about fitness and plan their own fitness program.	**PA 5.3** **Fitness** Actively participate in activities designed to promote health-related fitness, such as flexibility exercises and cardiorespiratory endurance activities.	**PA 5+.3** **Fitness** Investigate how different components of fitness contribute to the well-being of people at different stages of their lives.
	PA 4.4 **Participation** Plan strategies to ensure own ongoing participation in a variety of physical activities.	**PA 5.4** **Participation** Devise strategies to promote and encourage community involvement in physical activity.	**PA 5+.4** **Participation** Evaluate the factors that influence individual and community views on sport, recreation, and leisure.

Reprinted from Northern Territory Government, Department of Education and Training.

Queensland: End of Years 3 and 5

HEALTH AND PHYSICAL EDUCATION (HPE)	
By the end of year 3	**By the end of year 5**
Physical activity Fundamental movement skills are foundations of physical activity. • Students will improve their fundamental movement skills by becoming more mindful of their bodies and how they move through space. Improving these skills will lead to increased confidence in their physical performance. • Students will improve the quality of their performance in physical activity by developing their locomotor, nonlocomotor, and manipulative skills. Improving these skills promotes further physical activity participation. • Students will promote their health and well-being and continue to improve their movement skills by further participation in physical activity.	**Physical activity** Fundamental and simple specialized movement skills are elements of physical activity. • Students will improve their fundamental and simple specialized movement skills by applying the proper techniques. Application of these techniques will lead to a higher level of performance and more enjoyment when participating in physical activities. • Students will experience a higher degree of satisfaction when participating in either individual or group activities when they learn to work cooperatively, be aware of others, and play fairly. • Students will heighten their personal development, health and well-being, and movement capacity by further participation in physical activity.
Personal development Personal identity, self-management, and relationships develop through interactions in family and social contexts and shape personal development. • Students will learn that an individual's identity is formed by their unique personal qualities and life experiences. • Students will learn the importance of communicating effectively, taking others' feelings into consideration, and respecting differences in their relationships with their peers. • Students will learn that everyday life experiences and relationships bring about different reactions in themselves and others.	**Personal development** Personal identity, relationships, and self-management are influenced by beliefs, behaviors, and social factors and shape personal development. • Students will learn that an individual's identity is shaped by personality traits, interactions with others, and responsibilities and achievements. • Students will understand that portrayals of people, including stereotypes, impact the formation of a person's beliefs and attitudes about themselves and others. • Students will learn that group relationships and personal interactions are enhanced by exhibiting positive actions and showing respect for cultural practices.

Reprinted from Queensland Studies Authority 2007.

Queensland: End of Years 7 and 9

HEALTH AND PHYSICAL EDUCATION (HPE)	
By the end of year 7	**By the end of year 9**
Physical activity	**Physical activity**
Fundamental and specialized movement skills, movement concepts, tactics, and strategies are elements of physical activity.	Regular active and purposeful participation in physical activity promotes health and well-being and supports the achievement of goals.
• Students will learn to modify movement techniques and apply specialized movement concepts in order to improve their physical performance. Improving their performance will result in a more enjoyable physical activity experience. • Students will learn that perfecting teamwork, tactics, and strategies in a variety of settings will improve their movement capacities and performance and lead to greater enjoyment of physical activity. • Students will learn that participating regularly in physical activity leads to improvements in all facets of health-related fitness (cardio-respiratory endurance, muscular strength and endurance, flexibility).	• Students will learn how to apply movement concepts to help them develop and refine the specialized movement skills they need to assist them in improving their performance. Improving their performance will result in a more enjoyable physical activity experience. • Students will learn how to improve their performance and enrich their physical activity experience through the development of teamwork, tactical knowledge, and strategic thinking. • Students will learn how choosing physical activities that reflect their individual interests and goals along with the principles of training can heighten their performance abilities and improve their health and well-being.
Personal development	**Personal development**
Beliefs, behaviors and social and environmental factors influence relationships and self-management and shape personal development.	Diverse social, cultural, and environmental factors, values, beliefs, and behaviors influence relationships and self-management and shape personal development.
• Students will learn that a person's identity and self-image are affected by environmental factors (including media) and society's expectations of age, gender, and culture. • Students will learn to develop a positive identity and enhanced self-esteem by assuming of new roles and responsibilities, accepting leadership opportunities, displaying respect for different cultures and their practices, and working cooperatively with others. • Students will learn about strategies and personal and community resources that are available to help them navigate life circumstances and transitional events.	• Students will learn that a person's identity, health, and well-being are mutually dependent and that social and cultural experiences will have an impact on them. • Students will learn that establishing and maintaining productive relationships requires the use of effective communication skills, including thoughtful listening, considering other viewpoints, respecting cultural practices, and expressing ideas in a way that is sensitive to others. • Students will learn how the effective use of conflict resolution strategies, including negotiation, assists in the management of intrapersonal and interpersonal situations.

Reprinted from Queensland Studies Authority 2007.

South Australia: Standards 1 to 3

Standard 1	Standard 2	Standard 3
At standard 1, toward the end of year 2, the child . . .	At standard 2, toward the end of year 4, the student . . .	At standard 3, toward the end of year 6, the student . . .
1.3 Demonstrates a sense of self-worth and respect for others in social and working contexts and describes similarities and differences between themselves and others. [Id] [In] [C] [KC4]	2.3 Establishes a sense of self-worth in a variety of contexts within the school, and communicates personal feelings in different situations. [Id] [In] [C] [KC2]	3.3 Explains how different ways of describing people influence the way people value and treat themselves and others. [Id] [In] [T] [KC2]
1.5 Develops a range of capacities in social and working contexts by demonstrating skills of developing and maintaining effective relationships. [Id] [In] [C]	2.5 Understands different relationships and, through a variety of experiences, develops cooperative work and social skills. [Id] [In] [C] [KC1]	3.5 Assumes different roles when working as part of a cooperative group or team to achieve a shared goal and understands the effects on relationships. [Id] [In] [KC4]

Reprinted from South Australia Department for Education and Child Development 2001.

South Australia: Standards 4 to 5 and Beyond

Standard 4	Standard 5	Year 12 standards
At standard 4, toward the end of year 8, the student . . .	At standard 5, toward the end of year 10, the student . . .	
4.3 Investigates key ways in which groups and cultures contribute to forming identities. [Id] [In] [T] [KC1]	5.3 Analyzes the multiple identities they have in different contexts and with different people and appraises the social constructs of individuals and groups in the community. [Id] [In] [T] [KC1]	The year 12 standards for health and physical education comprise the capabilities of the essential learning demonstrated along with standards from external curriculum.
4.5 Develops skills for working effectively in groups and in teams, explores different constructions of group dynamics such as leadership, and identifies qualities for good leaders. [Id] [In] [KC1] [KC4] [KC6]	5.5 Critically analyzes the way individuals and groups use power to influence the behavior of others and how an imbalance of power affects individual and group identities. [Id] [In] [KC1]	

Reprinted from South Australia Department for Education and Child Development 2001.

Victoria

Health and Physical Education

- Engage in physical activity.

Interpersonal Development

- Building positive social relationships
- Working and learning in teams
- Managing and resolving conflicts

Personal Learning

- Can learn with peers, including by seeking and responding appropriately to feedback.
- Recognize and enact appropriate values within and beyond the school context.

Reprinted from Victorian Curriculum and Assessment Authority 2009.

Western Australia: K/P to Year 3

	K-10 OVERVIEW: SUGGESTED CONTEXTS AND TOPICS FOR HEALTH AND PHYSICAL EDUCATION			
Context	K/P	Year 1	Year 2	Year 3
Movement skills	**Fundamental movement skills** • Locomotor skills • Body management skills • Object control skills	**Fundamental movement skills** • Locomotor skills • Body management skills • Object control skills	**Fundamental movement skills** • Locomotor skills • Body management skills • Object control skills	**Fundamental movement skills** • Locomotor skills • Body management skills • Object control skills • Efficient techniques for fundamental movement skills
Strategies and tactics	Teacher-directed individual skills and strategies	Teacher-directed individual skills and strategies	Teacher-directed individual skills and strategies	• Awareness of direction of play • Strategies for individual activities
Playing the game	• Playing fairly • Sharing	• Taking turns • Cooperative play	Everybody's a part of the team	Safety considerations
Health-related fitness and recreation	• Daily fitness • Passive and active physical activities	• Daily fitness • Passive and active physical activities	• Daily fitness • Passive and active physical activities	• Daily fitness • Passive and active physical activities

Reprinted from Government of Western Australia Curriculum Council.

Western Australia: Years 4 to 7

	K-10 OVERVIEW: SUGGESTED CONTEXTS AND TOPICS FOR HEALTH AND PHYSICAL EDUCATION			
Context	Year 4	Year 5	Year 6	Year 7
Movement skills	Using fundamental movement skills in a modified game	Manipulating objects in a game situation	Moving to suit the game • Reading the play • Thinking players	Making movement decisions • Thinking players
Strategies and tactics	• Offense and defense • Skilled performance = game sense + technique	• Playing a position • Skilled performance = game sense + technique	• Creating and defending space • Skilled performance = game sense + technique	• Responding to different game situations • Player decisions
Playing the game	Fair play and playing by rules	Roles on the field or court	• Responsibilities as a player • Sportsmanship	Playing for the team
Health-related fitness and recreation	• Daily fitness • Physical activities for health • Lifelong physical activities	• Daily fitness • Physical activities for health • Lifelong physical activities	• Daily fitness • Physical activities for health • Lifelong physical activities	• Daily fitness • Physical activities for health • Lifelong physical activities

Reprinted from Government of Western Australia Curriculum Council.

Western Australia: Years 8 to 10

	K-10 OVERVIEW: SUGGESTED CONTEXTS AND TOPICS FOR HEALTH AND PHYSICAL EDUCATION		
Context	**Year 8**	**Year 9**	**Year 10**
Movement skills	Perform movement skills and sequences within different physical activities	Enhancing movement skills of their own and others	Specializing and modifying movement skills and sequences to optimize performance

Strategies and tactics	• Awareness of others and observing rules in play and simple games
	• Decision making in "off" play movement
	• Focusing play
		• Basic strategies and tactics applied to modified games
		• Using strategies and tactics to solve game problems
		• Shaping play
			• A range of strategies and tactics applied to changing conditions and situations
			  • Tactical questions
			  • Time, space, risk
			• Enhancing play

Playing the game	• Accepting the decision
	• Set codes of conduct
		• Playing a role
		  • Coaching, umpiring, player roles (attacking, defending)
		• Application of code of conduct and behavior
		• Sport education, teaching games for understanding, play practice
			• Range of roles
			  • Coaching, umpiring, player roles (attacking, defending)
			• Codes of behavior and conduct at various levels
			• Diversity
			• Sport education and play practice

Health-related fitness and recreation	• Activities that reduce sedentary time
	• Physical activity that promotes individual fitness
		• Recreating for personal enjoyment
		• Physical activities that contribute to the components of health-related fitness
		• Warm-ups
		  • Types
		  • Designing warm-ups
			• Recreating for life
			• Personal fitness profiles
			• Settings for exercise
			• Managing own healthy active lifestyles
			• Links to healthy active lifestyles
			• Community links

Reprinted from Government of Western Australia Curriculum Council.

Canada

Alberta Standards

Activity

- Acquire skills through a variety of developmentally appropriate movement activities; dance, games, types of gymnastics, individual activities; and activities in an alternative environment such as aquatics and outdoor pursuits.

Cooperation

- Interact positively with others.

Reprinted from Alberta Learning, Alberta, Canada 2000.

British Columbia Standards: K to Grade 3

	Kindergarten	Grade 1	Grade 2	Grade 3
Safety, fair play, and leadership	Safety guidelines for physical activity	Importance of safety guidelines	Safe behaviors	Safe behaviors
	Following rules and directions	Following instructions and safety guidelines	Following procedures and directions	Respect and encouragement for others during physical activity
	Working cooperatively with peers during physical activity	Working cooperatively with peers during physical activity	Respect for others during physical activity	Leadership in physical activities

Reprinted from British Columbia. Ministry of Education 2006.

British Columbia Standards: Grades 4 to 7

	Grade 4	Grade 5	Grade 6	Grade 7
Safety, fair play, and leadership	Safe participation in physical activity	• Leadership roles in physical activities • Importance of warm-up and cool-down activities	Safe procedures for specific physical activities	Safe procedures for specific physical activities
	Principles of fair play	Fair play in physical activity	Modeling fair play	Modeling fair play in all physical activities
	Leadership roles in physical activities	Leadership opportunities in physical activity	Respecting individual differences and abilities during physical activity	Contributing to a positive climate for physical activity

Reprinted from British Columbia. Ministry of Education 2008.

British Columbia Standards: Grades 8 to 10

	Grade 8	Grade 9	Grade 10
Safety, fair play, and leadership	Behaviors to reduce risk of injury	Safety procedures across the activity categories	• Safety procedures across the activity categories • Principles of first aid and emergency planning related to physical activities
	Dynamic warm-up activities and cool-down activities	Static and dynamic stretching in warm-up and cool-down activities	Warm-up and cool-down procedures
	Proper use of equipment and facilities	Proper use of equipment and facilities	Modeling proper use of equipment and facilities
	Respect for rules, teammates, opponents, and officials	Respect for rules, teammates, opponents, and officials	Respect for rules, teammates, opponents, and officials
	Etiquette and appropriate expression of emotion in physical activities	Etiquette and appropriate expression of emotion in physical activities	Etiquette and appropriate expression of emotion in physical activities
	Leadership in specific physical activities	Leadership in a range of physical activities	• Leadership in a range of physical activity situations • Officiating

Reprinted from British Columbia. Ministry of Education 2008.

British Columbia Standards: Grades 11 to 12

	Grade 11	Grade 12
Personal and social responsibility (leadership and community involvement)	*It is expected that students will . . .*	*It is expected that students will . . .*
	Describe and demonstrate qualities and problem-solving strategies required for leadership related to physical activity and recreation.	Consistently demonstrate safety practices in a variety of activities and environments.
	Demonstrate an understanding of the processes needed to coordinate events and programs in the school and community.	Adapt appropriate rules, routines, and procedures while involved in new and familiar activities.
	Demonstrate knowledge and skills required by recommended certification programs in selected areas related to physical activity.	Model self-respect and self-confidence while involved in physical activities
	Identify and describe the benefits of service and volunteer work in the school and community.	Apply appropriate interpersonal skills while organizing and participating in physical activities, showing respect for individual abilities, interests, gender, and cultural backgrounds.
	Identify and use appropriate technology when solving problems involving physical activity.	Consistently model fair play and etiquette in a variety of roles: • Performer • Coach • Official • Observer
	Demonstrate an understanding of the attributes required for pursuing careers related to physical activity.	Demonstrate the care and prevention of athletic injuries.

Reprinted from British Columbia. Ministry of Education 1997.

New Brunswick Standards

Reprinted from New Brunswick Curriculum Development 2000.

- Demonstrate efficient and effective movement skills and concepts
  - Locomotor skills
  - Nonlocomotor skills
  - Motor abilities
  - Manipulative skills
  - Body awareness
  - Qualities
  - Relationships
  - Spatial awareness
- Demonstrate an ability to cooperate with others.
  - Work with others to achieve common team goals.
  - Help others with learning by respecting their space and abilities and by coaching them when appropriate.
  - Provide good service to others (e.g., providing a good throw to allow a partner to practice catching).
- Understand the importance of safety rules and procedures.
  - Safety
  - Skills can be used in support of safety
- Develop positive personal and social behaviors and interpersonal relationships.
  - Fair play
  - Positive self-image
  - Cooperative learning skills
  - Nurturing behaviors
  - Leadership skills
- Develop a positive attitude toward active living in pursuit of lifelong health and well-being.
  - Physical activity is an enjoyable experience.
  - Physical fitness is a personal responsibility.

Ontario Standards: A1 to A3

	A1. Active participation	A2. Physical fitness	A3. Safety
Grade 1	A1.1 Participation in program activities, behaviors showing readiness [PS, IS]		A3.1 Behaviors and procedures that maximize safety of self and others [PS, IS]
Grade 2		A2.4 Personal and group goal setting related to physical activity [PS, IS, CT]	A3.2 Safety precautions for self and others, including those with medical conditions [PS, CT]
Grade 5			A3.2 Minimizing environmental health risks [PS, CT]

Reprinted from Ministry of Education, Ontario Canada 2010.

Ontario Standards: C1 to C3

Topic		C1. Understanding health concepts	C2. Making healthy choices	C3. Making connections for healthy living
Grade 1	Personal safety and injury prevention		C2.3 Caring and exploitive behaviors and feelings [IS]	
			C2.4 Safety at school [PS]	
Grade 2	Personal safety and injury prevention	C1.1 Personal safety: home and outdoors [PS]	C2.3 Standing up for yourself [PS, IS]	C3.1 Relating to others [IS]
Grade 3	Personal safety and injury prevention		C2.2 Safety guidelines outside of class [CT]	
Grade 4	Personal safety and injury prevention		C2.2 Decision making: assessing risk [CT]	
Grade 5	Personal safety and injury prevention			C3.2 Actions, self-concept [PS, IS]
Grade 6	Personal safety and injury prevention			C3.2 Responsibilities, risks: care for self and others, safety practices [PS, IS]
Grade 8	Personal safety and injury prevention	C1.2 Reducing risk of injuries, death [CT]		

Reprinted from Ministry of Education, Ontario Canada 2010.

England

Personal, Social, and Health Education Key Stage 1

Reprinted from Department for Education 2011. © Crown copyright.

Preparing to Play an Active Role as Citizens

2. Pupils should be taught the following:

   a. To take part in discussions with one other person and the whole class

   b. To take part in a simple debate about topical issues

   c. To recognize choices they can make and recognize the difference between right and wrong

   d. To agree and follow rules for their group and classroom and understand how rules help them

   e. To realize that people and other living things have needs and that they are responsible for meeting those needs

   f. That they belong to various groups and communities, such as family and school

   g. What improves and harms their local, natural, and built environments and about some of the ways people look after the environment

   h. To contribute to the life of the class and school

   i. To realize that money comes from different sources and can be used for different purposes

Developing Good Relationships and Respecting the Differences Between People

4. Pupils should be taught the following:

   a. To recognize how their behavior affects other people

   b. To listen to other people and play and work cooperatively

   c. To identify and respect the differences and similarities between people

   d. That family and friends should care for each other

   e. That there are different types of teasing and bullying, that bullying is wrong, and how to get help to deal with bullying

Cross-Reference to Physical Education: Knowledge and Understanding of Fitness and Health

4. Pupils should be taught the following:

   a. How important it is to be active

   b. To recognize and describe how their bodies feel during different activities

Personal, Social, and Health Education Key Stage 2

Developing Good Relationships and Respecting the Differences Between People

4. Pupils should be taught the following:

   a. That their actions affect themselves and others, to care about other people's feelings, and to try to see things from other points of view

   b. To think about the lives of people living in other places and times and people with different values and customs

   c. To be aware of different types of relationships, including marriage and those between friends and families, and to develop the skills to be effective in relationships

   d. To realize the nature and consequences of racism, teasing, bullying, and aggressive behaviors and how to respond to these situations and ask for help

   e. To recognize and challenge stereotypes

   f. That differences and similarities between people arise from a number of factors, including cultural, ethnic, racial, and religious diversity; gender; and disability

   g. Where individuals, families, and groups can get help and support

Cross Reference to Physical Education: Knowledge and Understanding of Fitness and Health

4. Pupils should be taught the following:

   a. How exercise affects the body in the short term

   b. To warm up and prepare appropriately for different activities

   c. Why physical activity is good for their health and well-being

   d. Why wearing appropriate clothing and being hygienic are good for their health and safety

Key Concepts of Physical Education Key Stage 3

1.1 Competence

   c. Responding with body and mind to the demands of an activity

   d. Adapting to a widening range of familiar and unfamiliar contexts

1.2 Performance

   c. Appreciating how to make adjustments and adaptations when performing in different contexts and when working individually, in groups, and in teams

   d. Understanding the nature of success in different types of activity

1.3 Creativity

    a. Using imaginative ways to express and communicate ideas, solve problems, and overcome challenges

1.4 Healthy, active lifestyles

    a. Understanding that physical activity contributes to the healthy functioning of the body and mind and is an essential component of a healthy lifestyle

    b. Recognizing that regular physical activity that is fit for its purpose, safe, and enjoyable has the greatest impact on physical, mental, and social well-being

Key Concepts of Personal Well-Being Key Stage 3

Reprinted from Department for Education 2011. © Crown copyright.

1.1 Personal identities

    a. Understanding that identity is affected by a range of factors, including a positive sense of self

    b. Recognizing that the way in which personal qualities, attitudes, skills, and achievements are evaluated affects confidence and self-esteem

    c. Understanding that self-esteem can change with personal circumstances, such as those associated with family and friendships, achievements, and employment

1.2 Healthy lifestyles

    a. Recognizing that healthy lifestyles and the well-being of self and others depend on information and making responsible choices

1.3 Risk

    a. Understanding risk in both positive and negative terms and understanding that individuals need to manage risk to themselves and others in a range of situations

    b. Developing the confidence to try new ideas and face challenges safely individually and in groups

1.4 Relationships

    a. Understanding that relationships affect everything we do in our lives and that relationship skills have to be learned and practiced

    b. Understanding that people have multiple roles and responsibilities in society and that making positive relationships and contributing to groups, teams, and communities is important

1.5 Diversity

    a. Appreciating that, in our communities, there are similarities as well as differences between people of different races, religions, cultures, abilities, and disabilities, sexes, ages, and sexual orientations

Key Concepts of Physical Education Key Stage 4

Reprinted from Department for Education 2011. © Crown copyright.

1.1 Competence

    a. Responding with body and mind to the demands of an activity

    b. Adapting to a widening range of familiar and unfamiliar contexts

1.2 Performance

    a. Appreciating how to make adjustments and adaptations when performing in different contexts and when working individually, in groups, and in teams

    b. Understanding the nature of success in different types of activities

1.3 Creativity

    a. Using imaginative ways to express and communicate ideas, solve problems, and overcome challenges

1.4 Healthy, active lifestyles

    a. Understanding that physical activity contributes to the healthy functioning of the body and mind and is an essential component of a healthy lifestyle

    b. Recognizing that regular physical activity that is fit for its purpose, safe, and enjoyable has the greatest impact on physical, mental, and social well-being

Key Concepts of Personal Well-Being Key Stage 4

Reprinted from Department for Education 2011. © Crown copyright.

1.1 Personal identities

    a. Understanding that identity is affected by a range of factors, including a positive sense of self

    b. Recognizing that the way in which personal qualities, attitudes, skills, and achievements are evaluated affects confidence and self-esteem

    c. Understanding that self-esteem can change with personal circumstances, such as those associated with family and friendships, achievement, and employment

1.2 Healthy lifestyles

    a. Recognizing that healthy lifestyles and the well-being of self and others depend on information and making responsible choices

1.3 Risk

    a. Understanding risk in both positive and negative terms and understanding that individuals need to manage risk to themselves and others in a range of personal and social situations

    c. Developing the confidence to try new ideas and face challenges safely individually and in groups

1.4 Relationships

    a. Understanding that relationships affect everything we do in our lives and that relationship skills have to be learned and practiced

    b. Understanding that people have multiple roles and responsibilities in society and that making positive relationships and contributing to groups, teams, and communities are important

1.5 Diversity

    a. Appreciating that, in our communities, there are similarities as well as differences between people of different races, religions, cultures, abilities and disabilities, sexes, ages, and sexual orientations

United States

Reprinted from National Association for Sport and Physical Education. (2004). *Moving into the future: National standards for physical education, 2nd ed.* Reston, VA: Author.

National Standard for Physical Education 1

Demonstrates competency in motor skills and movement patterns needed to perform a variety of physical activities.

National Standard for Physical Education 2

Demonstrates understanding of movement concepts, principles, strategies, and tactics as they apply to the learning and performance of physical activities.

National Standard for Physical Education 5

Exhibits responsible personal and social behavior that respects self and others in physical activity settings.

National Standard for Physical Education 6

Values physical activity for health, enjoyment, challenge, self-expression, and/or social interaction.

Low Activity Games

Low activity games are good to play when a group needs a rest or is ready to move more into mental activity. In these games, emphasis is on personal interaction, and often language is involved. Just how engaging these games can be is illustrated by my experience at a peace gathering in Valjevo, Serbia, where I taught a group of people how to play and lead New Games.

We were outside, and the local children were hanging around looking very curious, so I invited them to join us. I knew that the kids' enthusiasm would make the games more fun, and it would be good to have willing participants when my group practiced leading games.

The big breakthrough came one night when I led games around the town square with everyone at the conference. I invited the community people to participate. The kids and some of the adults joined in, but the most amazing thing was that the local men who did not join stayed and watched. And why was this so startling? Because this was the evening of the first football (soccer) match between Croatia and Serbia since the war had ended, and the men had been talking for days about the game. Yet they were so fascinated by what we were doing that they watched us instead of the football game. Knowing how crazy people in Europe are about football, and given the high emotions created by the recent war, I knew this was no small feat.

A What? 💿

Number of Players

10 to 20, but make another circle for more players. This size of group is especially good for young players who may get bored easily. Slightly larger groups work for older players.

When to Play the Game

Not recommended as a starting game because of the slow pace. A good game for a breather and a laugh.

Description of Game

Ka-mu-ni-kay-shon. Even simple messages get confused and muddled in the best of times, and this game is one of the best examples of that.

The group is usually sitting in a close circle. An object such as a pencil is passed around the circle by the leader, who starts by showing it to the first person while saying, "This is a banana." (Or anything else the leader chooses to say, as long as it is not "a pencil"!) The person replies in a startled manner, "A what?" "A banana," says the leader. The first person takes the pencil (or other object), turns to the second person, and shows them the pencil, repeating, "This is a banana." When the second person replies, "A what?" the first person turns back to the leader and asks again, "A what?" The leader once more informs the first person that it is "A banana," which the first person repeats to the second and passes the pencil. The second person shows the pencil to the third person in the same "This is a banana" manner, with the "A what?" response; the pencil and "A what?" travels back to the leader, who gives the "A banana" response, which, along with the pencil, travels back to the last person to hold the pencil.

The banana proceeds around the circle in this back-and-forth fashion. After about the fifth person, the leader sends another object such as a ball in the other direction in the same way, announcing, "This is an apple." The fun really begins when the two objects meet and cross. It is hysterical to watch people's expressions when they get confused about what to do and then completely lose it.

Safety Instructions

If someone other than you is designated the leader of this game, unless you know for sure it will not be a problem, remind that person that an object may not be called anything that will make others uncomfortable. Only good, clean fun is allowed. You don't need to worry much about physical danger—unless someone decides to use the pencil as a weapon! In that case, use something else. Also, if someone starts getting frustrated because he cannot say the right thing, tell them (1) it doesn't matter, or (2) to remember to pass only what the person next to him has told him. Do not try to think about what to say—it's dangerous!

Age Level

All. Making this game abstract, as in the original version, is confusing to youngsters. For younger players, only one object should be used to start, and it should be either the actual object or a picture of the object. This can be a great way to learn about objects they don't know about. For teens or adults, after they get the idea and have successfully passed two objects, try passing more than two objects to make it more challenging and interesting. If you want to increase the challenge still further, rather than passing the object back to the leader, pass just the question and answer, without having the object travel.

Equipment Needed

Some objects to pass around.

Location and Space Needed

Indoors or out, with enough room for a close circle of players, or more circles for more than 20 players.

Developmental Skills

Primary: self-control, verbal contact, adaptability, problem solving. Secondary: spontaneity, reaction, visual ability, cooperation.

Ain't No Flies on Us

Number of Players

5 to 50+.

When to Play the Game

In the middle of the session, when a breather is needed. Good as a tension breaker in a group where there are animosities.

Description of Game

This is an English teacher's favorite game. Just think of it: You get to use both a nonstandard word and a double negative all in six words. What economy! What a mess! Actually, this is a fun and funny way for a group to get out some tensions.

Two lines of people stand about 20 feet apart, facing each other. One line takes a step toward the other and quietly, calmly, and not too animatedly says this to them:

"There ain't no flies on us.

There ain't no flies on us.

There may be flies on you guys,

But there ain't no flies on us."

The other line then takes a step forward and says the same words back to the first line, but the second line is a little less calm, a bit louder, and slightly animated, making pointing gestures toward the other team on the "There may be flies on you guys" line and shaking their hands and heads on the "There ain't no flies on us" lines. Each line takes turns stepping closer, repeating the words while getting louder and more animated each time. When they get within an arm's reach of each other and each group has had its turn, ask everyone to stop, look around, and then shake hands to show no hard feelings, since (hopefully) there are no flies on anyone.

Safety Instructions

With kids and easily excited people, it is especially important to keep a distance between the lines, perhaps two arms' length, to avoid any overly physical interaction. In this case, to disperse aggressive feelings aroused by this game, follow it with a very active game.

Age Level

All. See safety instructions for presenting with kids.

Equipment Needed

None.

Location and Space Needed

Indoors or out, with room enough for two lines of players to be able to take at least three steps each.

Developmental Skills

Primary: verbal contact, adaptability. Secondary: self-control, spontaneity, cooperation.

Bloomps

Number of Players

10 to 35.

When to Play the Game

Any time after the first few games.

Description of Game

When something falls in the water, it makes a sound. Trying to represent that sound with a word does not really seem possible, at least not with total accuracy. But, given that, you are going to try to have some ducks, maybe even in a row, in the water.

Form a circle with your group. They can be seated, especially if the group is in need of a rest. Explain how when a duck lands, hitting the water, that sound is "bloomps!" Let the group know that they will repeat a word pattern. Then you can start by saying, "One duck." Going either to the left or to the right, the next person tells how many legs that duck has: "Two legs." The person after that says "Falls in the water," and the following person gives the designated sound for this, "Bloomps." Still going in the same direction, the next person in the circle says, "Two ducks," and the following person again tells how many legs they have: "Four legs," followed by the next person saying, "Fall in the water." For two ducks hitting the water, you have two bloomps, but they aren't given by the same person. So the next two people in the line say one "bloomps" each one right after the other. Then go on to three ducks, six legs, four ducks, eight legs, and so on, with the number of legs and persons saying "bloomps" changing each time.

Bloomps may not be the true sound of a duck landing, but you might learn something about simple multiplication and paying attention! Instead of ducks, try three-legged stools, any four-legged animal, or starfish for multiples of 3, 4, and 5. Depending on the age group, why stop there?

Safety Instructions

If someone gets confused about the number of ducks, legs, or bloomps she is at, offer help and encourage the group to do so as well. As if you could stop them!

Age Level

7 years and older.

Equipment Needed

None, but if you are sitting, you might want chairs.

Location and Space Needed

Indoors or out, with space enough for a circle of players.

Developmental Skills

Primary: verbal contact, multiplication. Secondary: spontaneity, self-control, problem solving, cooperation, creativity.

Bumpity, Bump, Bump, Bump

Number of Players

5 to 35.

When to Play the Game

Not necessarily the best game to start with, because it does single players out for embarrassment, even if slight. It's good to play after the group is a little loosened up and can laugh at their mistakes.

Description of Game

Are you afraid of things that go bump in the night? Just imagine how you will feel if they go bumpity, bump, bump, bump! Actually, there is nothing serious to be afraid of here, other than the embarrassment of not being able to think of a person's name quickly.

This is a circle name game. Each person in the circle asks the name of the player on the immediate left and right. The person in the middle (the pointer) will point at someone and say either "Left" or "Right" followed immediately by "Bumpity, bump, bump, bump." If the person pointed at names the person on the side called before the pointer finishes, the pointer moves on to someone else.

If the person pointed at does not say the name on time or gets it wrong, she changes places with the pointer. After the group gets the idea of the game and becomes good at it, add the command "Middle," which indicates naming the person who is pointing. If no one in the circle is making mistakes, have everyone in the circle change places to get next to someone else. A suggestion for groups of over 10: After the group starts getting good at naming people, you can increase the challenge by trying two people in the middle. Or three. Then watch the chaos!

Bumpity, Bump, Bump, Bump

Safety Instructions

Don't insist on someone going in the middle if they are uncomfortable.

Age Level

All. For young players, having a permanent adult in the middle would take the stress off answering incorrectly.

Equipment Needed

None.

Location and Space Needed

Indoors or out, all that is needed is enough space for the group to stand in a circle.

Developmental Skills

Primary: reaction, self-control. Secondary: verbal contact, adaptability, visual ability.

Captain Video

Number of Players

5 to 10; for more players, make two circles after demonstrating the game with the whole group.

When to Play the Game

When a group is tired and can use a little rest. Not a game recommended to start with a group of young people because it's too slow.

Description of Game

Everyone remembers Captain Video and his Space Rangers . . . oh, you don't? Well, not to worry. This game has nothing to do with that.

This game is played in a circle, and after you demonstrate how the game works with a few players, players face out from the center. To start the game, one player (at first, the person demonstrating the game) stands in the middle and taps someone on the back (everyone will be facing outward at this point). The second player turns around to face the middle to watch the first, who makes a simple movement or two and then takes the place of the second player in the circle, but now facing in toward the middle.

The second player does *not* repeat the movement immediately, but goes to a third player in the circle, taps them on the shoulder who turns around; the second player repeats the movements, remembering them to the best of his or her ability. This goes on from player to player until the last player turns around and is shown the movements. The last player and the first meet in the middle, stand back to back, and at the count of three do the movement so players can then see how much the movement has changed. To finish, the first and last player face each other and at the count of three do the movement again.

Then ask for a new leader to start some movements to pass. Make sure to emphasize not to make it too many movements. Suggest three at the most. You can usually do this game at least three times with a group before moving on. It is really fun to watch the movement change and change again. Once in a while, it even ends up changing back to the original movement!

Safety Instructions

None.

Age Level

8 years and older. Younger players should do only one movement, at least to start with.

Equipment Needed

None.

Location and Space Needed

Indoors or out, with enough space for everyone in the circle.

Developmental Skills

Primary: pantomime, visual ability. Secondary: adaptability, self-control, creativity, spontaneity.

Cows and Ducks

Number of Players

10 to 50.

When to Play the Game

Not really good as a beginning game because it involves closing the eyes, touching, and being touched by others; but it's superb as a game in the middle of the session to form groups. Okay as a closing game, but not terrific. A good preliminary game for building trust.

Description of Game

There are two kinds of people in the world: Cows and Ducks. Oh, yeah! Believe it. Well, in the game of Cows and Ducks there are, anyway.

Bring the players together in a fairly close circle. Each player has to decide whether he is a cow or a duck. You might allow a moment for introspection, but no longer! The goal is for all of each species to find and join others of the same species by linking arms. Each player must make the sound of his animal to locate others because everyone has their eyes closed. The game finishes when all the cows and ducks have found one another. In a place with obstacles, one or more players could be asked to keep their eyes open and watch over the others. If there are some who do not join the game itself, they could do this.

For small groups, the leader might go around and whisper in players' ears what they are, to ensure an equal number for each group. This is an excellent game for making teams or groups. If you do this game another time, feel free to have players select the animals and to choose more than two if several groups are needed. This gets to be fun when someone suggests an animal that doesn't make much of a sound or players don't know what sound it makes. "What sound does a giraffe make?" can always be answered with "If you are a giraffe, you already know!"

Safety Instructions

It may be good to have someone keep her eyes open to see that players don't violate the spirit of the game with roughhousing or inappropriate touching. As group leader, you should be watching if you anticipate any problems. Roughhousing is especially common with young players and boys of all ages; inappropriate touching is a possibility with adolescents. If at all possible, pick a place with few or no obstacles. This is a preliminary trust game.

Age Level

All. If very young players don't play the game quite right, they still can have a lot of fun.

Equipment Needed

None.

Location and Space Needed

Indoors or out, enough space so that players can walk around without crashing into obstacles.

Developmental Skills

Primary: tactile contact, adaptability, self-control, trust. Secondary: verbal contact, cooperation, problem solving, creativity.

Energy

Number of Players

10 to 20.

When to Play the Game

A good game to begin a session for adults. With teens and some young players, holding hands is a bit too much contact to begin with. A good preliminary trust game.

Description of Game

Here is a simple way to get the energy flowing in a group, from person to person.

The group forms a circle and each person takes the hand of the next person. Energy is passed from person to person as a gentle hand squeeze. After trying one direction, try the other. As a challenge, try both directions at once. Finally, try sending the energy in both directions with everyone's eyes closed. (Hint: As leader, after the squeezes have come back to you at least once, start a few extra energy squeezes to ensure an electric atmosphere.) After a while there is laughter, indicating that there is enough energy to move on to the next game.

Safety Instructions

This is normally considered a very gentle game, but some people, especially children, think that they have to squeeze hard to pass energy. Let the group know that the key is not how hard but how fast they send energy.

Age Level

5 years and older.

Equipment Needed

None.

Location and Space Needed

Room to fit everyone in a circle.

Developmental Skills

Primary: tactile contact, self-control, reaction. Secondary: cooperation, adaptability.

Face Pass

Number of Players

2 to 20, although with more than 10 young children it would be best to split into two groups (each with an adult) after explaining and demonstrating the game.

When to Play the Game

Sometime in the middle of a session, after the group has established a playful attitude. It's good to do it for a rest after an active game.

Description of Game

Here is a chance to get off the "serious squad," at least temporarily. Almost any attempt at a different face is met with laughter.

The players are arranged in a close circle. They can be seated, if desired. The leader starts by making a funny, dramatic, or unusual face, and then the leader passes this face to the next person, who must copy the face. Both then turn to show everyone else in the group the faces made. The second person then creates a new face to pass to a third person, following in the same direction. This continues around the circle until everyone has a turn. It's amazing what people will come up with, and even more so when a very serious person comes up with the most ridiculous face.

Safety Instructions

If someone is obviously having trouble coming up with a face to pass, let him know that he can say, "Pass," with the option to make a face at the end if he wishes. This will prevent embarrassment about participating in the game. On the other hand, you can encourage (not force) them to try, because it is great fun. Doing something quickly without thinking is probably the best way to cope.

Age Level

5 years and older, though with young players it would be better to split the group when there are more than 10 players; ideally have no more than 10 in a group after explaining and demonstrating the game. Additionally, with young players you might ask for volunteers to make a face and then have the whole group copy the face.

Equipment Needed

None.

Location and Space Needed

Indoors or out, with room enough for a close circle of players.

Developmental Skills

Primary: creativity, spontaneity, pantomime, adaptability, visual ability. Secondary: problem solving, self-control.

Four Corners

Number of Players

5 to 35.

When to Play the Game

Any time. Good rainy-day game.

Description of Game

Teachers love this game because it is quiet. It is fair enough for teachers to get relief from a noisy classroom. Noisy is not always bad; I have seen some very constructive classrooms that were pretty noisy. But sometimes it *is* nice to have quiet.

There are four corners that players can go to, each of which will be clearly identified with a number, 1 to 4. One player starts in the middle, closes her eyes, and counts slowly out loud to 10 while the other players quietly go to one of the corners. At that point, the person in the middle will call out the number of a corner. Everyone who is in that corner joins the middle person. One of them will be chosen as the new caller. Everyone can help count. The process is repeated until either one person or no one is left. At that point, the game can start again. Quietly. Hmmm, a nice experience. There is a new caller each time.

Safety Instructions

None.

Age Level

All.

Equipment Needed

None.

Location and Space Needed

Indoors or out. Room for players to move in a square. This is a great rainy-day game.

Developmental Skills

Primary: self-control. Secondary: creativity, problem solving.

The Last Detail

Number of Players

2 to 50+.

When to Play the Game

Better done in the middle of a games session, when a breather is needed, or when there is 5 minutes of time to fill.

Description of Game

Okay, eagle eye, just how observant are you? Want a chance to prove it? Well, here it is, sport, in spades. Yes, well. This game actually is an excellent opportunity to test your powers of observation or to improve them.

This game requires each player to have a partner. The game starts by having the partners face each other for a minute or so and observe each other to recall details about what the partner is wearing and how he or she is wearing it. Both partners turn away and change an agreed-on number of things (usually somewhere between three and six) that are visible to their partner, such as taking off a watch or putting a pen in a shirt pocket. Both people then turn to face each other to see if they can pick out the changes. So how did you do, sharp eyes?

Safety Instructions

None. If someone can't guess at all, perhaps have her try again and have her partner make changes that are readily noticeable.

Age Level

5 years and older. Younger players may need help deciding which things to change and may need to make obvious changes so that they are detectable.

Equipment Needed

Mostly what each person is already wearing.

Location and Space Needed

Indoors or out. Not much space needed, or what you have at hand.

Developmental Skills

Primary: visual ability, problem solving. Secondary: verbal contact, self-control.

Mnemonic Names

Number of Players

5 to 35.

When to Play the Game

Any time after the first few games. Because it may put a bit of pressure on a person, it is not good at the very start unless the group is relaxed or group members know each other very well.

Description of Game

If you're like me, remembering names is a major challenge. This game will give you a fun way to learn and retain other people's names. It's amazing how well the word associations help players remember each name.

First, have the group get in a standing or seated circle. Each person will, in turn, say something positive about himself that either begins with the same first letter (or sound) as his name, or something positive that rhymes with his name (in Dale's case, "Dynamic Dale" or "Dale Whale," respectively). The leader starts by saying something nice about himself, like "Dazzling Dale." Proceeding in one direction around the circle, the person next to Dale must then repeat what Dale said and also give herself a compliment. So Carol might say, "Dazzling Dale and Charismatic Carol."

Marty, the third person, then gives what the previous two people said about themselves plus a compliment to himself, such as "Dazzling Dale, Charismatic Carol, and Mature Marty." So it continues around the circle until everyone has had a turn. Don't forget to let players know that they will get help from the group if they need it. You can even remind them as the game goes on; this will reduce their anxiety level. When I play, I pay close attention to the names, because very often someone will say "Hey, Dale, now you name everyone!" and I'm ready.

Safety Instructions

Announce at the beginning that the group will help by giving hints (miming or verbal) or simply telling a name if someone is obviously having trouble. Set the example of doing so when someone gets stumped. The group will catch on and join in. The aim is to all learn names together and have fun, not to embarrass anyone.

Age Level

8 years and older. Younger players may find remembering too stressful, although they have surprised me on occasion. For teens, have the person use an adjective that says something positive about himself.

Equipment Needed

None.

Location and Space Needed

Enough room for players to form a circle.

Developmental Skills

Primary: verbal contact, self-control. Secondary: problem solving, creativity.

Partner Game

Number of Players

5 to 50+.

When to Play the Game

Any time partners are required, this game can be played beforehand to pair up players arbitrarily or even form teams.

Description of Game

Although this can be as simple as saying, "Everyone get a partner," you can make many variations on this theme. Because friends usually will take each other when this is said, you can separate them by saying other things like "Get a partner who has the same color shirt (or pants, shoes, sweater, socks)." Another way is to pick a physical feature such as color or kind of hair, color of eyes, or same or different sex.

You can also use month or season of birth, birthplace, or first or last initial of players' names. Or ask everyone to hold up one, two, or three fingers, and then take a partner who has the same number of digits extended. Or ask players to raise an arm, and then find a partner who has lifted the same arm. Or, still another way is to do the opposite of any of these to get the desired result. There are infinite possibilities; all you need to do is use your imagination. Teams can be made in the same way.

Partner Game

Safety Instructions
None.

Age Level
All.

Equipment Needed
None.

Location and Space Needed
Enough space is needed for the group to stand and move about.

Developmental Skills
Primary: cooperation, visual ability, reaction.

Pruie

Number of Players

5 to 35.

When to Play the Game

Not at all a starting game, this one requires a lot of touching and should therefore be done after a lot of preliminary trust activities. For groups that cannot handle that responsibility maturely, hold off on this one. It's a game to do near the end of a session, when the group needs a rest. Although it is not usually a problem, it may be wise to have someone watch over the group so that no players take inappropriate advantage of the situation.

Description of Game

We are all looking for something in life. Now, that something has a name, and it is Pruie. What, you may ask, is that? I could give a line of baloney about Pruie being mystical or some such nonsense, which if you have ever heard me explain the game live, I probably did. Or I can tell the truth, which is to say the Pruie doesn't mean anything. It's just for fun, like all New Games.

Pruie is a game where all players but one start as seekers. What everyone is trying to find is the Pruie, the thing that everyone blindly seeks. You might have everyone say the word *Pruie* together, because it is not a word people are familiar with. Or make up your own word. Why not!

One person is anonymously and secretly chosen as the Pruie. This can be done in a number of ways; here are two suggestions: First, the group leader can stay out of the game entirely by acting as a referee caring for the players' safety. This is a good idea if there are lots of hazards such as sharp edges or other obstacles in the space you are playing in. If this is the case, it's fun to start everyone moving about with eyes closed. The referee then whispers in someone's ear, "You're the Pruie!" The chosen person can then open her eyes.

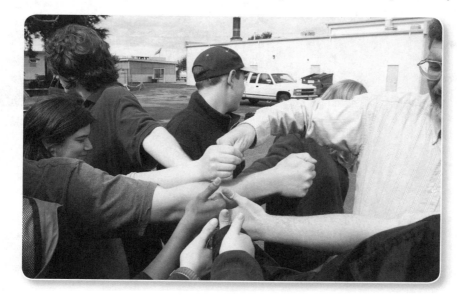

Alternatively, if there are no special hazards to watch for, the group leader can join the action (always recommended when possible). Then everyone can form a small circle, extend one arm in the center, and put their thumbs up. Players, including the group leader, close their eyes, and the leader finds a thumb to press down. The Pruie is thus chosen and opens her eyes. Then, while their eyes are closed, ask everyone to lower their arms, carefully step back a few paces, and begin to mill about in search of the Pruie.

You should demonstrate the following process before starting the game: When one person locates another person, they shake hands and one asks, "Pruie?" If the other person answers, "Pruie!" then it is *not* the Pruie. Only when you get no answer have you found the Pruie. (Pruies are like that. They say nothing, so you know it's them.) Not only have you found the Pruie, but you also now join hands with and become part of the Pruie, so if someone shakes your hand now, you do not reply and he joins as well. Seekers of the Pruie may find some part of it but need to find an open hand to join it. Therefore, if they find the middle, they must make their way to the end. The game ends when everyone has become part of the Pruie. You remember—that mystical, magical . . . .

Safety Instructions

You can ask either the Pruie or some person who is not participating to be safety guides to watch over Pruie seekers to keep them from crashing into walls, tripping over obstacles, or encountering similar fates.

Age Level

8 and older. For younger players the game as presented may be a little too abstract. Perhaps changing it to something like Teddy Bear or a name of their choosing could work.

Equipment Needed

None.

Location and Space Needed

Play in a cleared open space at least 15 by 15 feet (about 5 by 5 meters), or larger if the group is more than 10 people.

Developmental Skills

Primary: tactile contact; secondary: problem solving, verbal contact, adaptability, self-control, cooperation.

Sleeping Lions

Number of Players

10 to 35.

When to Play the Game

Not normally a game to start with because of its slow pace, but excellent for players needing a little rest. This can also be a good game for calming players down. Classroom teachers really appreciate that before starting their lessons.

Description of Game

You're not into harming animals? No problem. These lions are afflicted with sleeping sickness, and our job is to try to wake them up.

Everyone in the game is a lion except one person to start. Lions can sit, stand, or lie down and keep from being awakened by remaining completely still with the exception of breathing (please!), blinking and moving their eyes (it's fun to see what is happening to others), and occasionally swallowing. If the waker detects any other movement (other than the exceptions just named), even a smile, not only is the lion awakened, but he joins the waker in helping to wake other lions.

Lions must have their faces exposed and eyes open. Wakers may not touch the lions, or shout in their ears, or spit on them (when you do this game with kids, you have to cover all possibilities). Otherwise, wakers can do what they will to get lions to move. Usually the best strategy is to say something that will get the lions to laugh, and all a waker needs is to get a lion to smile. If any lions last more than a few minutes, they can be declared sleeping lions and applauded to finish the game. If a sleeping lion can move without the waker(s) seeing him, that's fine, which adds another dimension to the game.

Safety Instructions

Wakers often try to violate the rules to get lions to move, so be aware that this can happen, and discourage it when you see it.

Age Level

All.

Equipment Needed

None.

Location and Space Needed

You need just enough space for the group to spread out a bit.

Developmental Skills

Primary: self-control, creativity, problem solving. Secondary: adaptability, pantomime.

Sun Monarch

Number of Players

10 to 35.

When to Play the Game

Any time, usually not first or last but okay for these, too.

Description of Game

I don't know why this game is called Sun Monarch. The name it had when I found it was Sun King in Germany, but I changed it so it was not gender specific. Beyond that, I have not found a better name. Yet. (But now that it is here in print . . .) Maybe you can come up with a better name. After all, this is an excellent game for stimulating the imagination.

The game is pretty simple, can be educational, and is always fun. Have the group stand at one end of the room or in a line, if outside. Stand beside the group on a place marker or, if in a room, in the middle of it, roughly 10 feet away. To start, simply say, "I am the sun." Once that is done, encourage two people to come forward (one on either side of you), face the group, and tell something that relates to the sun, such as "I am the light" or "I am the heat." It can also be the opposite, like "I am the dark" or "I am the cold." Finally, it can be other meanings of the word or the sound of the word. For instance, sun could be interpreted as "son" so that a person could say, "father," "sister," or some similar relative.

Once there are two people on either side of you (or your original sun), pick one of them and both of you go to the opposite side of the room from where the group is gathered. The person who is left behind gets to be the new caller, and that person gets on the place marker and repeats what he or she had said

(for instance, "light"). Now two more people can come up from those who have not yet had a chance, get on either side of the caller, and give two new words that relate to the word "light," such as "bright" or "bulb." The middle person arbitrarily chooses one, and the process continues until everyone has had a turn. It usually helps to have a marker that the middle person can move on to, so it is clear who the new caller is each time.

Now, just to make this terribly relevant to education, you can take any subject matter and ask players to use words that relate to it. You can write words from your latest chapter or subject you are studying. It all works.

Safety Instructions

If you can see someone truly is stumped and left at the end, save them embarrassment by letting those who have already gone have another turn.

Age Level

5 years and older.

Equipment Needed

A place marker for the caller, but this can easily be improvised. A piece of scrap paper will do.

Location and Space Needed

Indoors or out. Room enough for the group to move from one side to another.

Developmental Skills

Primary: creativity, problem solving, verbal contact. Secondary: reaction, self-control, spontaneity.

This Is My Nose

Number of Players

5 to 35.

When to Play the Game

After participants get used to each other and the idea of playing these games. This also makes a good time filler, and it's a possible ending game.

Description of Game

Some people are confused about many things, and if you saw this game without knowing what was going on, you would be convinced the players were more than just a little off kilter. But, in fact, you have to work very hard at keeping things straight to act confused in such a manner. Clear?

This game can be played with partners, but this explanation is for a group in a circle. One player starts by pointing at any appropriate place on his body other than his nose—his shoulder, for instance—and saying, "This is my nose." No, he is not nuts, but proposing a challenge. What the next person in the circle needs to do is point at some place other than her shoulder (knee, for instance) while saying, "This is my shoulder," or the place the first person pointed to. The process repeats with the next person, who says, "This is my knee," which the second person pointed at, while pointing somewhere else—his eye, for instance.

The point for each succeeding person is to say what the preceding person pointed to while pointing to something else on himself or herself. Naturally, if some players are baffled by this (it will happen!), take time to go through it with them until they get it. As I mentioned, this can also be played with partners to

see who gets confused first. Confused? Congratulations. You should be. If the group gets proficient at this, to add challenge, ask them to speed up. Sooner or later they'll blow it, but what fun!

Safety Instructions

You might make an agreement beforehand to declare certain parts of the body off limits to avoid embarrassment for players.

Age Level

8 years and older. You might change the game for very young players, who might have fun pointing at the part of the body and naming it correctly, each one naming a new part. This might be challenging enough for them!

Equipment Needed

Place markers (optional)

Location and Space Needed

Indoors or out. Only enough space needed for a circle of players.

Developmental Skills

Primary: problem solving, verbal contact, adaptability. Secondary: self-control, visual ability, creativity.

Three-Syllable Game

Number of Players

5 to 50+.

When to Play the Game

A good game for sometime in the middle of a session. It is a little complex to be a starting game, and it puts a little too much stress on a couple of people a bit early to be the first game.

Description of Game

Thanks to Gudrun from Germany for this game. This activity is a real challenge, but at the same time it is quite a lot of fun. When people get the right three syllables of a word, but in the wrong order, and can't figure out the word, or get the right syllables in the *right* order and *still* can't get the word, it is hilarious. I have seen players get nearly hysterical with laughter when the guessers are so close but can't quite guess the word.

When presenting the game, make sure everyone knows that a syllable is part of a word. This is particularly true for younger or foreign players. Give examples, like syll-a-ble or ba-na-na. Ask your group for a few examples. To demonstrate the game, choose a three-syllable word and divide the group into three equal

groups at least 10 feet apart in the shape of a triangle, each taking a syllable. Then, ask each group to say their syllable one time all together at the count of three.

Next, ask a few (two or three) players to volunteer to be guessers, and ask them to go out of earshot. The rest of the players pick a new three-syllable word and divide into three groups again, as described.

The guessers return, standing exactly in the middle of the three groups. One of them counts to three, at the end of which all three groups say their syllables all together at the same time. The guessers talk together to see if they can get the word. If not, they can move closer to one group or another, count to three again, have the groups repeat their syllable, and have the guessers try again. The process is repeated until the word is found. It is a stitch to watch the guessers get the syllables, but not figure out how to put them together and to get excited with them when they do.

Safety Instructions
None.

Age Level
6 and older. For kids age six or seven use two-syllable words to begin, as a way to teach what syllables are and to learn how to do the game. With teens, after they understand the game, you can introduce more challenge by trying four-syllable words.

Equipment Needed
None.

Location and Space Needed
You need enough room for players to divide into three groups, 10 feet apart.

Developmental Skills
Primary: problem solving, cooperation, verbal contact, creativity. Secondary: self-control, spontaneity.

Um-Ah

Number of Players

2 to 50+.

When to Play the Game

In the middle of a session, when a comic breather is needed. *Not* a game you would normally start with, unless the group knows each other well and is relaxed and open to try anything.

Description of Game

Ah, but the nights are long in Scandinavia in winter. All they have to do to keep themselves occupied is invent silly songs to sing. And here is a prime example. This is a song that, as far as I know, comes from Norway. At least that is where I came across it and learned it while giving a workshop in the early 1980s. Three grown men sang it to me and had me in stitches—it was so funny watching them. The words are as follows:

"Um-ah," said the little green frog one day. "Um-ah," said the little green frog.

"Um-ah," said the little green frog one day, and stuck his tongue out, "Um-ah, um-ah, um-ah-ah."

The thing about the "Um" is that when you sing it, you close your eyes and scrunch up your face, while the "ah" is done with eyes wide open and tongue stuck way out. That's really all there is to it. It is definitely silly and good for a little tension reliever. Here is the whole song:

"Um- ah!" said the lit - tle green frog one day. "Um- ah!" said the lit - tle green frog.

"Um- ah!" said the lit - tle green frog one day, and stuck his tongue out. "Um-ah! Um-ah! Um- ah ah!"

Got it? Grab it. Gribbet, gribbet.

Safety Instructions

None. Well, not exactly. If this game is introduced before a group is ready for it, it could turn them off for any other games. So make sure the group is warmed up, or loose and ready to try something a bit weird. Okay, maybe a little bit *more* weird.

Age Level

All.

Equipment Needed

None.

Location and Space Needed

You do not need much space—only space enough for a group standing together.

Developmental Skills

Primary: pantomime. Secondary: cooperation, verbal contact.

Zip, Zap, Pop

Number of Players

5 to 20. For more players, make two or more groups after demonstrating how the game works.

When to Play the Game

In the middle of the session, when the group needs a rest, or when something a little different is called for.

Description of Game

Who needs snap, crackle, and pop when you have zip, zap, pop? The group sits together in a close circle. The first thing to pass around is a zip, which is accomplished by placing a hand on top of the head with the fingers pointing at the person on one side while saying, "Zip." The person on that side also puts a hand on top of his or her head with fingers pointing in the same direction while saying, "Zip." It passes from person to person this way around the circle. Practice this in one direction and then the other.

The next thing to learn is a zap, which is done by putting the hand under the chin the opposite direction from which a zip is coming. A zap makes a zip reverse directions. And, of course, if one zaps a zap, the zip re-reverses directions. With me so far? A pop is done by pointing to anyone in the circle, who then has to either start passing a zip, zap it back, or pop to someone else.

After the leader starts a zip, it is up to the person who receives it whether to pass it, zap it, or pop it. And so it goes, around the circle one way, then the other, or maybe jumping across, at the whim of whoever is the latest receiver. The faster it goes, the sillier it gets! Got it? Get it!

Safety Instructions

None.

Age Level

8 and older, although a simplified version can be played with those younger by just doing "zip," and later, when they get that, a zap.

Equipment Needed

None.

Location and Space Needed

Enough space is needed for a circle of players.

Developmental Skills

Primary: reaction, self-control. Secondary: cooperation, spontaneity, creativity, visual ability, problem solving, pantomime.

Zoom ⊙

Number of Players

5 to 35.

When to Play the Game

A truly great game to start or finish a session. Being in a circle, players have a good sense of one another. The game is not physically threatening or too silly to begin with. It can be done anytime.

Description of Game

Got no car? No problem. Zoom will give you the means to move about your group and still have a laugh.

After having players form a close circle, pass the sound "zoom" from person to person around the circle. After doing that, suggest to the group that the sound is actually a car, and that it travels by being passed from person to person. You can use several gears or speeds to demonstrate how the speed increases with each gear.

Finally, introduce brakes, making a screeching sound while pulling your arms up as if holding tightly on the steering wheel while extending the right leg forward as if applying car brakes. This not only stops the zoom, but makes it go in reverse. Practice brakes as a group. Then, zoom away. Suggestion: Allow only one use of brakes per person, especially with a large group or with children. Don't worry too much about having to remember if a person has braked before. The group will be quick to point it out, and if someone does brake more than once, so what?

There have been times that groups have changed Zoom to make it even more interesting. When one group applied the brakes, they reversed the spelling of zoom as well to become Mooz. While working with a handicapped group in South Africa, the clients changed Zoom to Soen (not sure of the spelling), which meant kiss! Changes like this make a game fun!

Safety Instructions

None.

Age Level

All. For preschoolers or other very young players, introduce at stages. What happens with brakes may be hard for them to understand at first.

Equipment Needed

None.

Location and Space Needed

Enough space is needed for a circle of players.

Developmental Skills

Primary: self-control. Secondary: reaction, pantomime, cooperation, problem solving, verbal contact.

Chapter

Low/Moderate Activity Games

Games that are not quite at a low activity level and have a bit of animation but are not quite at a moderate level are, well, low/moderate activity games. I know, how clever! I was introduced to one of these, Quack!, while at a conference in Geneva, Switzerland. The presenters for the conference were meeting to get to know one another, and an English fellow named Jim got up and started with this game. It involved people walking backward while bent at the waist. When two people bumped into each another, they stopped, lined up butt to butt, and bent down to look between their legs. When they made eye contact, they both said, "Quack!"

This was a most outrageous thing to do and see: a roomful of people bumping and quacking. I would previously never have started with such a silly game, but this was the right group to try it with; it worked! And so I added a game to my repertoire and an experience to my knowledge. Here, I offer it, and many others, to you.

A Day at the Races

Number of Players

5 to 50+.

When to Play the Game

Any time.

Description of Game

This game is not based on the famous Marx Brothers comedy film from the 1930s, although you may end up having quite a few laughs.

Arrange the group in a close circle, seated on their knees. Ask everyone to imagine that they are on a horse and are about to be in a race. There are certain commands that the group will respond to from the narrator or race caller. When the riders are galloping, they make brief, quick bobs up and down. For making a right turn or a left turn, everyone leans in that direction. When riders come to a fence or water, the riders lift their bodies up fully on their knees and go back down. As riders approach the home stretch, the bobbing up and down speeds up. Then there are the cameras to record the finish, transforming riders into camera persons (that is, arranging their hands as if they were holding a camera recording the horses as they go by at the finish).

The race caller says something like what you would hear at the track: "And they're off! It's Breakaway taking the early lead, followed by Knobby Knees and Whirlaway. They're coming to the first turn, and they turn left. Now they're coming to a water hole, and up! And over. And the race is on, with Nose Beam edging into the lead. They're approaching a fence, and up! And over they go. . . ."

Just reading the description is nowhere near as exciting as playing this game. It's really fun and a lot of laughs. And everybody wins the race.

Safety Instructions

For someone with wonky knees, this would not be a good game to play. As presenter, you might let players know that if they have bad knees, this might not be a game for them unless they sit on their bottoms or on a chair. (This mostly applies to young adults and older.) It's best played on a soft surface like grass or carpeting.

Age Level

5 and older. Might be difficult for the elderly.

Equipment Needed

None.

Location and Space Needed

In or outdoors, on a soft surface if at all possible. There must be room enough for a tight circle of players.

Developmental Skills

Primary: pantomime, tactile contact, balance. Secondary: leaning on, skillfulness and coordination, self-control, adaptability.

Amoeba

Number of Players

5 to 50+. For groups larger than 15, make more than one amoeba.

When to Play the Game

This has too much physical contact to be a starting game. While it could be a game for finishing, the most useful time would be in the middle or near the end of a session.

Description of Game

An amoeba is a one-celled organism. But because it is made up of molecules, we can represent that in the form of a game. Well, okay, this is all an excuse for a giant hug, but, hey, we have to keep our academic standards!

Get your groups in a huddle, and have some group members form a cell wall by linking arms in a circle facing out around the outside of the group so that everyone is very close together. Once they are formed, have your amoeba do a little wandering about the area you are in. This can be quite fun by itself.

Just for fun, you might want to have a race. Designate a starting line where the group can line up, and let them know where the finish line is. If you have enough players for two or more groups, you can have them race against one another. If you have only enough players for one group, you can have them race against themselves, having them race more than once to see if they can improve their time. The length of the course depends on the space you have, but a minimum-length race would be 20 feet (6.5 meters) and a maximum length would be 100 feet (30 meters).

It is not a serious race (how could it be!), so see that players take care that they do not hurt one another trying to win.

Safety Instructions

Since everyone is crowded together, some players may feel a bit overwhelmed and uncomfortable. If they indicate that they do not want to play this game, allow them to watch at first; if you see that someone is uncomfortable, even if he does not say anything, let the person know individually that he can sit out the game if he chooses. One thing that may allow the person to be more comfortable is to ask them if they want to be on the outside ring of people who are holding hands to contain the group. The other problem that might arise is that some players may try to take the game too seriously as a race and damage others in the process. To overcome this, before starting the game, ask everyone who wishes to play to agree to

- yell, "Stop!" if things become too rough or uncomfortable for them, or
- stop if anyone else yells, "Stop."

And you are there to see that they live up to their promise!

Age Level

8 years and older. Probably possible with younger students, but it could get too hectic and become Make a Pile. That might be okay if no one is hurt.

Equipment Needed

None.

Location and Space Needed

Whether indoors or out, enough space is needed for the groups to be able to go a little distance for a race, at least 20 feet.

Developmental Skills

Primary: cooperation, problem solving, verbal contact, tactile contact; self-control. Secondary: adaptability, spontaneity, visual ability.

A Rum Sum Sum

Number of Players

5 to 50+.

When to Play the Game

This game is a good starter or closer with young children, but it's better to present in the middle with adults and teens.

Description of Game

When I was traveling and teaching in Sweden, I came across this game that I had never seen before. Later I also encountered it in Germany in a slightly different form, and still later in the United States where several people claimed they played it in Scouts or youth groups. Whatever. It's a fun activity for all ages.

This game is a song with hand movements. Start seated in a close circle, facing in. The tune is almost a monotone "A rum sum sum" sung while alternating hand pats to the knees. "Goody, goodies" are sung while alternating hand pats to the chest, a pat for each goody. "A-rah-man" is sung while extending arms over the head and bringing the arms down. After the group has grasped the tune, try to go faster, and then faster again. Try Information Age speed—as fast as you can go! To calm the group down, go very, very slow. The words are as follows:

A rum sum sum, a rum sum sum;

Goody, goody, goody, goody, goody, rum sum sum. (Repeat.)

A-rah-man, a-rah-man.

Goody, goody, goody, goody, goody, Rum sum sum. (Repeat to finish.)

Safety Instructions

This is intended to be a gentle game. If you know people who have back problems, they should not bend too far forward on the "A-rah-man" chorus. They should know this, but a reminder is always helpful.

Age Level

This not the first game to do with teens, who would think it too silly or childish initially. Later on, when they are open to trying New Games, it can and usually does work, especially when the game is speeded up. Little kids love this game.

Equipment Needed

None.

Location and Space Needed

You need enough space for the group to be able to sit in a circle. Hint: Do not ask the group to sit on dirty or wet grass unless they are dressed for it.

Developmental Skills

Primary: skillfulness and coordination. Secondary: cooperation.

Bear Hunt

Number of Players

5 to 50+.

When to Play the Game

Not usually a starting game with teens or adults, but it could be fun to start with for younger players.

Description of Game

Generally this game is played in a close-seated circle. Rather than try to describe the game, it may be easier to tell participants to follow your movements and repeat after you. You start by "marching" through the woods using alternating hand slaps to the legs. Along the way, you encounter a few obstacles: a bridge, a mountain, and a swamp. These are negotiated by crossing the bridge with hand slaps to the floor, climbing the mountain by grasping upward in the air as if climbing, and squishing through the mud of the swamp by moving your arms as if tromping through the mud. The words to the chant are as follows:

Chorus

At the beginning and between each verse. If you want to, you can sing the first three lines (see the music), or you can just chant them rhythmically, like the verses:

> Goin' on a bear hunt!
> Gonna find a big one!
> Gotta keep moving!
> It'll be fun!

Verses

> There's a bridge up ahead.
> Can't go around it.
> Can't go under it.
> Gotta go over it.

(Repeat the verse after each recurrence of chorus, only substitute "mountain" for "bridge" during the first repetition, and "swamp" for "bridge" and "through" for "over" on the second repetition.)

At long last, we find a cave with something in it with the following chant:

> There's a cave up ahead. [Slow the hand slaps down.]
> It's all dark inside. [Slowly wave arms in the air, like groping in the dark.]
> Here's something furry . . . [Act as if you feel something with your hands.]
> . . . and big! [Move arms apart, to show how big it is.]

OH! It's A BEAR! [Run out of cave, rapid hand slaps to the legs.]

Run home going through or over the obstacles in reverse order. The leader will say each obstacle as the group gets to it, such as "Through the swamp!" accompanied by rapid squishy swamp noises. After passing an obstacle, return to "running" hand slaps.

When you get home, you are safe and the game is over. Now don't you wish it would be that easy to escape from a real bear?

Leader: Go - in' on a bear hunt!
Group: Go - in' on a bear hunt!
Leader: Gonna find a big one!
Group: Gon - na find a big one!
Leader: Got - ta keep mov - in'!
Group: Got - ta keep mov - in'!
(Spoken): It'll be fun!

Safety Instructions

None.

Age Level

This is not a game that a leader would ordinarily start with for a group of teens. It may seem too childish for them. Ordinarily, only after the group is used to playing the games would they be ready for this.

Equipment Needed

None.

Location and Space Needed

Indoors or out, with only enough clear space for a circle of (usually) seated players.

Developmental Skills

Primary: skillfulness and coordination, verbal contact, adaptability. Secondary: visual ability, cooperation, self-control.

Elephant, Rabbit, Palm Tree 🔘

Number of Players

10 to 35.

Suggestion: With a group of more than 15, add more than one player in the middle after the group understands the game.

When to Play the Game

This is not usually a good game to start off with, because if someone gets stuck in the middle he may get a bit embarrassed. It would be better if done after a few warm-up games or in the middle of a session.

Description of Game

We are going on a walk into fantasy land. No, not the Walt Dizzy kind. We might see many things, but for certain we are going to see elephants, rabbits, and palm trees, each made from groups of three players in a pose.

It works like this: The group starts in a circle with a player in the middle. The player in the middle points at someone in the circle and says, "Elephant," "Rabbit," or "Palm tree." If the person pointed at is told elephant, that person makes an elephant trunk, and the two people on either side of the person pointed at make huge ears for the elephant by using their arms. If the person is

told rabbit, the person pointed at makes bunny arms and teeth, while the two players next to him make long rabbit ears on the side of the middle person's head by using their hands or forearms. Finally, if the person is told palm tree, he or she makes a palm tree trunk with branches sticking up in the air, and the two on the side make palm branches sticking out.

The player in the middle who is pointing counts (at first to five, but after the group gets good, only to three) while the threesome is forming. After the count, the threesome can let the formation go. If one of the three is too slow, or gets it wrong, she takes the place of the person in the middle. Suggestion: As the group improves, add other animals such as donkey, where none of the threesome moves. (Donkeys are stubborn and do not like to move!) Have the group create other possibilities. The quicker the middle person is, the more likely she will catch someone off guard. It is priceless to see someone in the circle forget to move and then belatedly realize that she is now the new pointer.

Safety Instructions

None.

Age Level

For young players, start with only two elements of the game (such as rabbit and palm tree), or for very young players, only one. Add on as players understand what is required. For teens and older, add on as many new elements as they can handle and invent to add to the challenge and excitement.

Equipment Needed

None.

Location and Space Needed

Enough room is needed for a circle of the players with no obstructions in the middle.

Developmental Skills

Primary: reaction, pantomime. Secondary: problem solving, tactile contact, adaptability, self-control, creativity, visual ability, skillfulness and coordination.

Huddle Up

Number of Players

10 to 50+.

When to Play the Game

Not usually a game to start with because of the touching and hugging. See safety instructions about this matter. This is a good, random way to form groups or teams when these are needed. If there are certain players you want to split up, pick something to form groups so that they are put in different groups (e.g., group by shirt color if they have different-colored shirts). A good game to start for developing trust.

Description of Game

I first learned this game in England where it was called Huggy Bear. I'm in favor of anything that encourages hugs, but kids and especially teens may be put off by the mere suggestion of closeness—so I changed the name to Huddle Up. It's a great game to learn about other people in the group, such as where they were born or if they had brothers and sisters.

To start, ask the group to mingle about in and around one another until the leader says, "Huddle up," plus something to organize players into groups, such as "Huddle up, (color of shirt)." In this case, all those with the same-colored shirts or tops quickly assemble in a huddle, arms around one another. Once everyone has found the proper group, the leader tells them to mingle again until the next call.

After the leader makes a few calls, he or she can invite others to make the call. Imagination is the only limitation. Other examples of calls include season (or month) of the year you were born, type or color of hair, color of clothes, everyone who has skin! (Yes, that is one big hug with everyone.)

Safety Instructions

Some people are not inclined to hug, so you may need to change the game to having groups hold hands or stand in a circle to make the game socially acceptable. This is especially true with some groups of adolescents.

Age Level

All.

Equipment Needed

None.

Location and Space Needed

Enough room for the group to mingle about.

Developmental Skills

Primary: Tactile contact, creativity, reaction. Secondary: verbal contact, spontaneity, cooperation, visual ability.

Human Spring

Number of Players

2 to 50+.

When to Play the Game

Sometime in the middle of a session.

Description of Game

Cooperation. What is in a word? What does it mean? Here is how to learn what the word means experientially. For this game, players absolutely must cooperate for it to work. To not do so would be like a house of cards that someone blows on. It collapses, and so will you without complete cooperation.

Each player gets a partner of about the same size. They stand facing their partner, one arm's length apart, feet together. After putting their hands up to their chests with palms outward, they fall forward, catch each other by the hands, and push back upright without losing their balance. The pair must keep their bodies stiff. Then they move back a foot each and try again. The first times it's easy, but it gets more difficult and more frightening quickly. The distance they move apart can be made smaller.

The idea is for partners to keep in balance with each other, even when they push back up (keeping their feet together makes it more challenging). They need not go so far that they fall on their faces. Any time they feel they have gone as far as they would like, let them know they can stop. To do this game successfully, a person must learn cooperation.

Safety Instructions

Remind the players to leave enough space between couples so that they do not fall into each other.

Age Level

8 years and older.

Equipment Needed

None.

Location and Space Needed

Indoors or out. Best if played on a soft surface like carpeting, mats, or grass, but not required.

Developmental Skills

Primary: cooperation, trust, verbal contact, self-control, strength, leaning on. Secondary: tactile contact, adaptability, balance, visual ability, skillfulness and coordination.

Knights, Mounts, Cavaliers

Number of Players

10 to 50.

When to Play the Game

Good in the middle of a session.

Description of Game

Even if you have never been enamored by the era of knights and the like, you can enjoy this game. It could possibly be called Rush Hour because it often seems like organized chaos. Call it what you will, it is fun and challenging, whatever your role.

Players have a partner, and if someone does not have a partner, he or she is a floater. Even if everyone has a partner, ask one pair to volunteer to be floaters. The partners and floaters move around the space independently of one another to music until the person who starts the music stops it and yells out one of the following words: *knights*, *mounts*, or *cavaliers*. Partners must then find each other and assume the form for the call, with no direction of which partner assumes which role, which must be spontaneously decided.

For knights, one person is on one knee while their partner, who is standing and facing the kneeling person, extends a

sword (hand) to the knight's shoulder. For mounts, one person is on all fours, and the partner sits on the other as if he were a horse. For cavaliers, one partner gets on one knee while the other partner sits on the other knee. The last partners to do the command become floaters. Floaters attempt to obstruct partners from getting to each other without touching. The round of the game ends when there is only one pair of partners left. These words of description just can't do justice to this game. It's great fun.

Safety Instructions

It is important for floaters to maintain the nontouching aspect of this game, so if people violate this rule, remind them. If that does not work, asking them to sit out a round usually works. You might remind people with bad backs to ask their partners not to sit on them for the mounts.

Age Level

5 years and older. Younger players may need only two elements to start with; older players may enjoy inventing new ones after they understand the game.

Equipment Needed

A CD or tape player and music, although if someone can sing or hum, the equipment is not necessary.

Location and Space Needed

Indoors or out. Room is needed for participants to move around.

Developmental Skills

Primary: self-control, reaction, adaptability, visual ability. Secondary: verbal contact, tactile contact, cooperation, problem solving, creativity, spontaneity, pantomime, balance, leaning on.

Knots and Giant Knot 💿

Number of Players

5 to 10 for one small knot, although if there are 12 or more players, you can make two groups. Up to 50 can play Giant Knot.

When to Play the Game

A good opening game for a small group of adults. Teens and children may be resistant to the touching and proximity of other players. However, after a few games when young players relax a bit, this is a good preliminary trust activity.

Description of Game

Here is a good metaphor for representing a group that is experiencing complications. We literally represent this by getting knotted up physically.

A circle of players starts by standing close together facing in. They put their hands in a clump on top of one another in the middle and start mingling them. Everyone can then close their eyes and, when told, find two hands to clasp. Upon opening their eyes, check to see that all players have two different hands. To add challenge, see that players do not keep the hand of a person next to them. Players, without losing contact by hand, although not necessarily with a tight grip, try to untangle into a circle. Facing in or out does not matter.

If the knot is insoluble, allow the players to pick one grip to let go and reconnect in a better way. Then the players can see if they can unwind the knot. If not, have the group choose another grip to undo and redo. They can continue in this manner until the knot is solved. This way, there is no knot that cannot be unwound. After doing this with a group, everyone will feel a lot more comfortable with one another.

With more players, make more than one circle. Or have the whole group hold hands in a circle to start, and then have them tangle by going under or over arms without letting go of hands to form a Giant Knot. When players cannot move any more, start to unwind. This way, having started in a circle, you always end in a circle. This works with as many as 50 people.

Safety Instructions

Remind players that if they start to feel their wrists or arms getting twisted, they need not maintain a hand clasp but merely need to keep touching. Also, remind everyone that if they are being hurt, they can simply say, "Stop," and everyone will stop, thereby avoiding a painful situation.

Age Level

With players under 8 years of age, this can easily become a modified game of Tug of War or Make a Pile. As long as no one is getting hurt, that is no problem. Sometimes leaders have to let go of their expectations of what is supposed to happen.

Equipment Needed

None.

Location and Space Needed

Enough room for a circle of players.

Developmental Skills

Primary: problem solving, tactile contact, cooperation, skillfulness and coordination. Secondary: verbal contact, adaptability, self-control, creativity, visual ability, trust, balance, climbing.

Lap Game

Number of Players

5 to 50+.

When to Play the Game

A great closing game to bring a sense of unity to the group but can be used in the middle of the session, too. Preliminary trust games should be done before attempting this.

Description of Game

My friend Todd Strong, coauthor of *Parachute Games,* says that during Napoleon's time, soldiers were looking for a way to rest without freezing in the winter. Someone thought of sitting on one another's knees in a circle, thus avoiding sitting on the cold ground. This seems pretty farfetched to me, so I think Todd was taking poetic license. To tell the truth, I have no idea where this game came from. I can only remember trying to help organize about 2,000 people in a lap-sit in 1976. In fact, that was kind of boring; people had to wait about 20 minutes while it all got organized. It is much more fun to have a smaller group of people who can all hear someone giving them instructions so that they can all sit at the same time.

We first get the group into a very tight standing circle facing in so that each person is touching the person next to him or her. Everyone takes a quarter turn in the same direction so that each person is facing the back of a person. (This is often the hardest part. Invariably, several players turn the opposite way.)

Each player puts the hands on the hips of the player in front of him or her. It is important to get the proper spacing. If everyone's arms are stretched out, people are too far away from one another and they need to take a step in toward the center. If people are too close, they need to take a step out from the center.

Try small step adjustments first. The idea is to be able to sit on the knees of the person in back of you while having the person in front of you sit on your knees. Having someone sit on your thighs is painful!

At the count of three, you might try having everyone touch down briefly to see if they are all connecting properly. Then have the group all sit on others' knees all at the same time, perhaps with the magic words "On my knees, please."

When seated, for a challenge, you might suggest walking together. In this case, everyone needs to move the same leg at the same time. Stand up together to finish—you might say something like "Off my knees, please." Not very Napoleonic, but it works.

Safety Instructions

Before starting, ask if anyone has serious knee problems. They may want to stay out of the game if it seems as if it will be too stressful. It is good to do this on a soft surface because the circle sometimes collapses.

Age Level

Younger players might have trouble touching and might be a bit too silly to do this successfully. If they are having fun and nobody is getting hurt, that is okay.

Equipment Needed

None.

Location and Space Needed

Enough room for a seated circle, preferably on a soft surface.

Developmental Skills

Primary: cooperation, self-control, balance. Secondary: tactile contact, adaptability, skillfulness and coordination.

Look Up

Number of Players

10 to 50.

When to Play the Game

When a slow-down activity is needed. This can be a starting game even though having to look someone in the eye may prove threatening for some people. It may work okay as a finishing game, though.

Description of Game

This game defines the word *simplicity*, and it is a game that nearly everyone can do. It's also surprisingly fun. You can't imagine it by just reading the description. You have to do it. So, do it!

There are two circles of players. One person is chosen in each circle to be the caller who starts by saying, "Look down." Everyone looks down at their feet. When the caller says, "Look up!" everyone looks up directly at someone else in that circle. (No fair looking around!) If two people are looking at each other, they both go to the other circle. If the caller leaves the circle, a new caller is chosen. There is something magical about being in a circle and have someone return your look. It's surprising and delightful.

Safety Instructions

If the group is shy, do not start with this game. Wait until the group gets more relaxed.

Age Level

All players, down to age 3, should be able to understand this game.

Equipment Needed

None.

Location and Space Needed

Indoors or out. Very minimal space required for two circles.

Developmental Skills

Primary: reaction, visual ability. Secondary: cooperation, adaptability, self-control, spontaneity.

Musical Chairs Unlimited (or Musical Chairs Forever)

Number of Players

5 to 50 (numbers not at the extremes are best).

When to Play the Game

Middle of a session; could be a good closer, too.

Description of Game

Everybody knows Musical Chairs. You play, you get eliminated, you feel bad. You feel even worse if you are first out. But no more! Here, it is as much fun to not find a chair as it is to find one. Maybe more fun. Mostly, you don't end up feeling like a bozo having to watch others have fun while you sit and stew, eliminated.

Basically, this is Musical Chairs where no one gets eliminated. We start with a circle of chairs facing outward, with one fewer chair than players. Music is put on, and when it is turned off, usually after about 10 to 15 seconds, everyone finds a chair. The one person who does not find a chair is not out, but simply finds someone with a chair and sits on his or her knees. A chair is removed each time the music starts until there is one chair that everyone ends up sitting on. And no one feels bad, at least not for being left out.

Safety Instructions

Although there is no penalty for not finding a chair, some players may still feel they have to get one by any means. Perhaps this may be solved by allowing walking only or some other way to slow the game down, if there is a problem.

Age Level

3 years and older.

Equipment Needed

Enough chairs or removable place markers that a player can sit on and some means of making music. Live singing or humming will do, if necessary.

Location and Space Needed

Indoors is best, but it can be done outdoors with removable place markers.

Developmental Skills

Primary: tactile contact, self-control, reaction, balance. Secondary: cooperation, visual ability, speed, adaptability, endurance, skillfulness and coordination.

Name Echo 🔘

Number of Players

5 to 35.

When to Play the Game

A good game to use near the beginning for adults, maybe even first if the group is not too shy. However, if the group is a bit wary to participate, this game may draw too much attention to each member. In that case, it would be best to introduce this game later, when the group has begun to relax and have fun. Then they will be ready and responsive. Timing is important.

Description of Game

Here is a chance for every person to get group recognition by hearing her name repeated in unison by the group while doing some kind of movement. It also happens to be a pretty good way to learn names.

First, form a circle. Each person will have an opportunity to introduce his name by saying, shouting, singing, whispering, or breaking it into syllables—or whatever way they can think of. Each person also does a movement, something everyone can do. Then the name and movement are echoed back by the circle of players. Indicate which direction you will go in the circle. Start by introducing your own name. Each person will take a turn introducing his name in his own unique way. Will you remember every name? Perhaps not, but some will surely stick.

Safety Instructions

Some players are (or think they are) gymnasts, so indicate that the movement should not be something only they or a few can do—such as a flip or a split. It should be something everyone in the group can do. Even a forward roll may not appeal to those over 30.

Age Level

All. Young players may prove shy with so much attention on them, so let them know that if they are stumped or too embarrassed, they can say, "Pass." However, ask at the end of the game if they'd like a chance to present their name.

Equipment Needed

None.

Location and Space Needed

Indoors or out, with enough room for a circle of players.

Developmental Skills

Primary: creativity, spontaneity. Secondary: pantomime, visual ability, adaptability, self-control, cooperation, verbal contact, skillfulness and coordination.

Quack! 💿

Number of Players

2 to 35.

When to Play the Game

This game could be considered a bit silly. As such, it is not usually a game to begin with, especially with adolescents, who would rather die than look uncool. Unless the group is very venturesome to start with (such groups do exist), this is a game that would be introduced only after the group has relaxed and loosened up quite a bit. At that point, the game can be a catalyst for opening up the group much more. This is a good trust-building game.

Description of Game

There is silly and then there is Quack! This game rates about a 10 (out of 10) on the goofy scale, but when introduced at the right time, it really opens a group up to help them grow closer.

Players put their hands on their knees and walk slowly backward. When a player bumps into someone, both line up rump to rump, bend over, look at each other from between their legs, and when their eyes make contact, they greet each other with "Quack!" Then, each person moves on and repeats with another person. This game lasts only a few minutes at most. How could you not feel closer to others after doing that together?

Safety Instructions

Advise people to keep their heads up while walking backward to avoid getting dizzy and to keep from getting bumped by another player. Remind everyone to move carefully to avoid potentially painful collisions, especially involving the head and neck. For psychological safety, see the comments in the When to Play the Game section.

Age Level

All. It may be difficult for some players to bend over. Therefore, adapt as needed. You might just have them line up rump to rump and say, "Quack" when they bump, without bending over.

Equipment Needed

None.

Location and Space Needed

As I have indicated, this is a very silly-looking game, so players might prefer to be someplace where they will not be seen by onlookers. Of course, there are always those who *would* want to be seen. Otherwise, not a great deal of space is needed—enough for the group to stand in and bend forward somewhat.

Developmental Skills

Primary: balance, tactile contact. Secondary: verbal contact, skillfulness and coordination, visual ability, leaning on.

Rain Game

Number of Players

5 to 50+.

When to Play the Game

A great game to begin or end with, or for any time. It is nonthreatening and interesting, and people of all ages can participate.

Description of Game

Okay, okay, I do not really know if this game allows you to control the weather, but very often when a group did it, it rained within hours. You be the judge.

The group starts in a circle, with the leader initiating and passing sounds to create a rainstorm. Each player keeps making a sound until the next one comes around. The sounds start quietly, get louder, and then become quieter again.

Some of the sounds include finger tapping (two fingers from each hand), chest thumping (open hands), foot stamping, thigh slapping, hand clapping, hip slapping, finger snapping, tongue clucking, hand rubbing, and shushing.

As the last sound you pass comes back to you, you can make a comment to end the game, such as how the group is attracting the rain (or sun, in which case it becomes the Anti-Rain Game). For doing the game a second time, I suggest having players close their eyes. It slows the game down, and it's okay if someone peeks to see if the new sound has arrived. It will amaze players how much it does sound like a rainstorm. The change in perception of not having their eyes and having to rely on their ears is an interesting aspect as well. Remember, if you only believe!

Safety Instructions

None.

Age Level

All.

Equipment Needed

None.

Location and Space Needed

Only room enough to create a circle to include all players.

Developmental Skills

Primary: cooperation, self-control, skillfulness and coordination. Secondary: adaptability, pantomime, and visual ability.

Robots

Number of Players

5 to 50+.

When to Play the Game

Although this game can be done at any time, because there is incidental touching, you should do it after a few games that have less touching. It is a good preliminary trust activity.

Description of Game

We may be moving into a robotic age, but it will never look like this. What happens here is pretty chaotic, but it is a riot.

Have everyone form groups of three (or if there are one or two players left, a few groups of four), and have them pick one person as a robot controller for the others in each group, who become robots. Robots, when set in motion, go in a straight line. When a robot encounters another robot, a boundary, or an obstacle of any kind, it stops and makes a warning sound. Before starting, the group decides on their unique warning sound so that the controller knows his or her robots need assistance.

Upon hearing the warning sound, the controller rushes to the aid of the robot, turning it in a new direction. Once a robot stops, it cannot start again even if the obstacle is gone. After a minute or so, have groups get together again and pick a new controller and perhaps a new sound or word. To add a little spice to the end of the game, have the last round of robots move at double the speed they have been going. Remind them not to damage other robots. If you thought it was a madhouse before this, you will now have mass hysteria. But in a fun way.

Safety Instructions

Remind players (robots) that although they may have collisions, they should not try to hurt one another. After all, robots who are damaged may need to go to the repair shop (a time-out). This is especially true when robots speed up, so you need to know your group well enough to know whether they are mature enough to handle increasing speed. If they can't handle the speed, keep slowing them down until the game is safe.

Age Level

5 years and older. Younger players can do this, but possibly with only one robot.

Equipment Needed

None. Boundary markers can be improvised.

Location and Space Needed

A fairly clear space large enough for robots to move about, but not too large—having robots encounter each other is a big part of the fun of this game.

Developmental Skills

Primary: verbal contact, tactile contact. Secondary: self-control, creativity, cooperation.

Sardines

Number of Players

5 to 20.

When to Play the Game

When you have a lot of places that people can hide, and they need a slow game that can last a long while. It is best played in the dark, but need not be if there are enough good large hiding places.

Description of Game

This is the most absolutely fantastic version of Hide and Seek I know. Unfortunately, I don't get to do it often because the conditions need to be right, and it can take a long time to play. But I love to play it when possible.

First, the group is gathered together. One player is selected to go and hide within an agreed-on area with defined "no go" places. While the person goes off to hide, the others count to a certain number, say 25 or 50, however much time is deemed appropriate to be able to hide. While counting, the group does not look, and I even suggest they close their eyes, giving the person hiding a chance to hide close to the group.

When they are finished counting, the group spreads out to look for the player who is hiding. When they find the person, they can hide with him or her. They might not want to do so immediately if they are being watched, but they might go away and come back when no one is looking. Those who are searching need to keep an eye on the others, noting as well as possible when and where someone disappears. Eventually, everyone ends up with the original one who hid. Usually, as more players begin to find the original one who hid, they tend to get noisier, thereby attracting other seekers.

Safety Instructions

If the last players are having trouble finding the hiding group, the group should give hints, like making little sounds, to help the seekers. This will keep seekers from getting frustrated and feeling bad.

Age Level

6 years and older. Younger or immature players should either team up with an older player or be given more hints or help, especially when they are the last ones left (see safety instructions).

Equipment Needed

None.

Location and Space Needed

Indoors or out. A place with lots of nooks and crannies where players can hide all at once.

Developmental Skills

Primary: problem solving, visual ability, tactile contact, cooperation. Secondary: verbal contact, self-control, adaptability, creativity, spontaneity, pantomime, balance, climbing, leaning on, crawling.

Say Something Nice

Number of Players

5 to 35.

When to Play the Game

Any time. Good finishing game for young children.

Description of Game

We all like to hear compliments once in a while, even if we secretly know we are wonderful. This game guarantees everyone will hear something good about himself or herself.

Have everyone sit in a circle. Then either throw, pass, or roll a Nerf ball to someone else in the circle and give that person a compliment. No repeats to persons are allowed until everyone has had the ball and a compliment. Ask the group to try to give different compliments each time. That's it! It just feels good for someone to acknowledge you!

Safety Instructions

Everyone needs to be included for each round. Sarcastic compliments are not acceptable—if someone makes one, he or she will miss one round.

Age Level

5 and older. Preteens and teens usually need preliminary games as a warm-up to relax for this or it may seem too personal. With young children you may need to discuss what things could be said.

Equipment Needed

A soft ball that is easy to catch; Nerf or foam balls are good.

Location and Space Needed

Indoors or out. An open space big enough for the group.

Developmental Skills

Primary: verbal contact, visual ability, throwing and catching, cooperation.
Secondary: problem solving, adaptability, self-control, creativity, spontaneity, skillfulness and coordination, reaction.

Sleeper

Number of Players

10 to 35.

When to Play the Game

Any time in the middle of a games session, especially when the players need a breather. Also can be used as a time filler.

Description of Game

This game actually used to be known as Killer, but every so often someone was offended by that title—hence the reinvented title with more or less the same game. Whatever you want to call it, the game is a good one for guessing. By the way, kids usually love the title Killer, but it's your choice.

Someone is chosen secretly as the sandman or sandwoman who winks at other players to put them to sleep. The group starts by walking around the room looking into one another's eyes. The sandman tries to covertly wink at people. When someone has been winked at, they do not immediately fall into a slumber.

They walk for at least another five steps—to give the sandman a fair chance to get away—before giving a loud yawn and stretch and drifting off to slumberland, either by lying down on the floor or sitting down on a chair.

The group tries to catch and thereby stop the sandman. After all, it's not bedtime! If someone thinks he knows who the sandman is, he announces loudly, "Stop!" while raising his arm.

When everyone has stopped, the accuser points out the sandman or woman. If correct, the sandperson falls asleep. If not correct, the accuser must nod off. The game continues until all are sleeping or the sandman is caught.

For those who cannot wink, or just for variety, the signal that someone has been put to sleep can be something else. For instance, everyone can be shaking hands and the sandman can be rubbing his index finger on the wrist of a person to put her to sleep. Also, to add challenge to the game, you can announce that two people have to agree to make an accusation, but they cannot talk to each other about who they will accuse. They must say, "Stop," count to three, and make their accusation, all in unison. If they say the same name, and it is the sandman or woman, that person must, of course, fall asleep. But if the two accusers blame two different people for being the sandman (even if one of those is correct!), or blame the same person but are wrong, the accusers must both fall asleep.

A variation of this game is called Sleeping Sickness. When a player starts to fall asleep, anyone they touch on the way down also falls asleep.

Safety Instructions

None.

Age Level

8 years and older.

Equipment Needed

None.

Location and Space Needed

Great indoor game, but also can be played outdoors. Room enough for players to mingle.

Developmental Skills

Primary: problem solving, visual ability, pantomime. Secondary: cooperation, verbal contact, adaptability.

Spiral

Number of Players

10 to 35.

When to Play the Game

A great game to end on for bringing people together. Probably too much touching and physical closeness to be used early on for most groups.

Description of Game

Have you ever needed a really big hug? Here is your opportunity to get just that, though more so for some than others.

The players start in a circle holding hands. When we find a volunteer, the person lets go of one of the two people holding his hands. He moves into the middle of the circle, not letting go of the other person's hand and, while remaining stationary, becomes the center of a spiral. Meanwhile, the person whose hand he let go of leads the rest of the linked line wrapping not too tightly around the volunteer center person creating the spiral. While wrapping around, the group can sing a song everyone knows, such as "Row, Row, Row Your Boat." Depending on the group, once they are wrapped up, ask everyone to let out a sound of how they feel right then at the count of three.

To get out of the spiral, you could just let go of hands. But don't. That's too easy. You could unwrap opposite the way you wound up. But don't. Too boring. There is another way. For that, start by having the center person lead the group out without letting go of hands. You can kindly raise your arms a bit to allow the person to duck under and out. Or not.

Safety Instructions

Sometimes the group wraps too tightly, causing either psychological stress or physical pain for those already in the spiral. Make sure this does not happen. This is more likely to happen if the group runs or quickly makes the spiral, so watch for this. One result of the group's winding too tight is that they lose their balance and fall over. This can be all right if no one is getting hurt.

Age Level

8 years and older.

Equipment Needed

None.

Location and Space Needed

Indoors or out. Enough unobstructed room for a circle (even if small) of people holding hands.

Developmental Skills

Primary: tactile contact, self-control, cooperation. Secondary: adaptability, balance, verbal contact, leaning on, skillfulness and coordination.

Chapter 5

Moderate Activity Games

One of the times I did a keynote presentation at a conference for a thousand people, I did the game Choo Choo (described on page 128). It is a game where I start off by acting like a steam locomotive, stop in front of someone, and give him a cheer. The person I stop in front of joins me in a line, and then we go off and find someone else. After a few people joined the train, I saw that people were looking at me skeptically. I could see they thought I was going to add people one at a time until everyone was a part of it. They thought I was bonkers. I smiled to myself, because I knew what was coming. After the train got to be seven people long, I split it into two trains. I did this again when the trains got to about seven people, and I kept doing it. It was a raucous scene at the end of the game, with 20 trains cheering someone's name. I loved the irony: A game that looked as if it would take hours took about 10 minutes. And every person that wanted one got a cheer.

Car-Car

Number of Players

6 to 50+.

When to Play the Game

Although this game could be the first one introduced with the right group (one where group members are very familiar with one another), it is usually not the first game to start out with, because it requires a fair amount of trust. It can normally be introduced near the beginning after a group rapport is established. It is a good preliminary trust game because it does involve a low level of trust.

Description of Game

Okay. You zoomed around the racetrack a while with your car and found that your brakes worked just fine in the game Zoom (see pages 76-77). Now it is time to take that baby out on the road for a spin. It's time for Car-Car. You don't have a license? No problem. In this game, everyone has a universal New Games license to drive.

Players are asked to pair up by height (if someone is left over, there can be a group of three). Partners stand within an arm's length facing the same direction, one in front of the other. The one in front is the car, the one in back is the driver (clever, huh?). The car must put her arms up in front of herself in a relaxed manner, with hands open at about waist level, creating bumpers.

The car closes her eyes and the driver, with eyes open, puts his hands on her shoulders and begins to guide the car carefully, avoiding crashing into other cars. After a few minutes, everyone stops and switches: Car becomes driver, driver becomes car. So if you are the driver first, you had better treat your car right if you expect similar treatment.

Safety Instructions

It is very easy for children of all ages to change this game into bumper cars or demolition derby. That is okay as long as it is not too rough, but if it gets too rough, perhaps a police car can be introduced to stop people and give them tickets, or you could have a tow truck to tow crashed cars to the garage where they must stay for at least a minute for repairs. Or, you can simply stop the activity and ask the group for a suggestion so that no one will get hurt. If there are vast discrepancies in size, you might remind very large cars to be very aware of any minis on the road to keep the little ones safe.

Age Level

All.

Equipment Needed

None.

Location and Space Needed

A space large enough so that everyone can move around.

Developmental Skills

Primary: visual ability, balance, self-control. Secondary: reaction, cooperation, tactile contact, adaptability, creativity, pantomime, skillfulness and coordination.

Car Wash

Number of Players

5 to 35, although for 25 or more players make two or more car washes, as needed.

When to Play the Game

Not usually a game to start a session, since there is a lot of touching involved. Normally, a group needs at least some time playing together to accept being touched so much. You should do other preliminary trust games before doing this one as well.

Description of Game

So. You have just been zooming about in your Car-Car (see pages 122-123), and it has gotten all dirty. Never fear, Car Wash is here.

The players form two parallel lines facing each other, about three feet apart. They can kneel, crouch, or stand, depending on the softness of the surface and the inclination of the participants. Ask the players to practice the motions a car wash makes, such as spraying, brushing, and towel drying. Then tell them that they are going to *be* the car wash (and the cars, for that matter).

Each car (player) gets an opportunity to say what kind of car he is and the kind of cleaning he needs—vigorous or gentle, depending on the condition he is in. For instance, an old Chevy that has been driving through mud will need a lot of cleaning, but a new Bentley right off the showroom floor will need only light dusting.

Just for fun, we can have a fantasy car wash where players can be anything they want: a frog, a double-decker bus, even a cat on a hot tin roof. Whatever.

Safety Instructions

Some players are a little over-whelmed by the touching involved in this game. If it is obvious that a player does not want to take a turn being a car—she may hesitate or look very uncomfortable when it is her turn—let her know that she can say, "Pass" and continue in the game.

Although this is meant to be a gentle game, some groups get a little too enthusiastic with their "washing." Let the cars know that they can say, "Stop" so that the activity stops. If you see the car is being damaged, have everyone stop, and remind the players in the car wash that if they are not careful, their insurance rates for repairing ravaged vehicles will skyrocket. If this playful approach is not sufficient, simply tell players to be less rough, or ask for suggestions to become more gentle.

Age Level

All.

Equipment Needed

None.

Location and Space Needed

Room for two lines of players. On a soft surface such as carpeting, mats, or grass if played on the knees. As players reach the end of the car wash and join, it will grow on the end. If you have very little space, have both sides of the car wash move back toward the starting point.

Developmental Skills

Primary: tactile contact, leaning on, crawling, self-control, creativity. Secondary: trust, pantomime, spontaneity, skill and coordination, cooperation.

Caterpillar

Number of Players

5 to 35. For every 25 players, make new lines.

When to Play the Game

Not a game to begin with for the usual group, especially if they do not know one another well. Playing this game requires that a fair amount of trust already be established. This game is best played after a series of games have been played, including a number of introductory trust games. In fact, it may take several games sessions before a group would try this game. They might need weeks or even months to be ready for it. Some groups who are open for anything could try it the first session as the first game. You must sense the group's readiness, and if you're wrong, simply end the game and suggest another less threatening one.

Description of Game

A caterpillar has that weird way of moving where part of the body bulges at one end (I think it is the front) and looks like the bulge moves along the length of its body. Very strange. This game is called Caterpillar because it resembles this movement.

Have your group form a line or lines, depending on the numbers, all facing one direction. Then have them all lie down on their bellies so that their heads are about even and close enough to one another so that they touch at the hips and shoulders. Arms are out in front of them, either to rest their heads on or to extend in front of them. Have the person at one end of the line roll on to the person next to them, and have them continue on down the close-packed line as if rolling on a human carpet. The result looks a bit like a caterpillar. Take turns by having the next person in the line go until everyone who wants to try has had a chance. Check periodically to see that there's enough space at the end of the line so that the next roller can lie down there when she is done. You may need to move the line down occasionally to accommodate everyone. Make

sure the players in line are close together, or the player rolling will fall in the gap and get stuck. In the end, players may not feel much like a caterpillar by doing this game, but it is fun rolling on others and being on the bottom getting squished.

Safety Instructions

The player rolling must not use his elbows to turn so the players lying under him don't get elbows dug into them, which is painful. Make sure the person rolling stays in the middle of the players beneath. That is, the rolling person should have his head near the head level of the line. If he rolls too high, he will bang heads; too low and he will be on the legs and backs of knees, which is painful. If this starts to happen, have the roller stop and move back squarely on top of fellow players. Game leaders should be standing and help move the person rolling back to the correct place, if needed. A soft surface is needed to keep players in the line from feeling too much pain.

Age Level

8 years and older. The game can be done with players of mixed ages, half of whom are significantly older. Younger players can then be fit in between older players so that they do not take the full weight of an adult player.

Equipment Needed

If played indoors, mats, carpeting, or some other soft surface.

Location and Space Needed

Room for one line of players. Indoors or out, if played on grass.

Developmental Skills

Primary: tactile contact, self-control. Secondary: skillfulness and coordination, strength, cooperation, verbal contact, leaning on.

Choo Choo (Name Train) 💿

Number of Players

10 to 50+.

When to Play the Game

Not a game to start with normally because players may feel silly doing it, but after a group has begun to open up and relax by playing together and building up some trust, this is a game that can really lower the barriers of the groups' inhibitions. When players see this game, they often literally fall over laughing. After this game, they will be ready for almost anything.

Description of Game

Trains are not only a good form of transportation, they are also good places to meet people. And on this train, you can meet a lot of people who will cheer your name.

The game starts in a circle. The leader, after explaining that it is a name game that is easier to do than to explain, starts chugging along moving and sounding like a steam engine. He stops in front of a person, asks her name, and then gives her a little cheer using her name, such as "Edna, Edna, Edna Edna Edna!" At the same time, he also makes body movements, which may vary with each added person. The leader then invites the person to join the train by turning his back to her and putting her hands on his waist (or shoulders). Once a person joins the train, she can make train sounds and motions, too.

When they come to the next person, Aaron, they ask his name and when they hear it, they both give a cheer together, "Aaron, Aaron, Aaron Aaron Aaron!" Aaron is asked to join and the game continues. Another way is when the train comes to a new person, each person in the train gives their name first.

After the train has about six or seven people, split the train in two. You can do this when you have a couple cars behind you. Since you are in the middle of the train, just break from the front of the train when it has grown to about three players long and form a new train. For a large group, repeat splitting as many times as necessary until everyone is given a cheer within a few minutes. This game may bring back train trips as a preferred means of travel. Oh, yeah!

Safety Instructions

As stated, players will likely be embarrassed if this game is introduced too early.

Age Level

8 years and older.

Equipment Needed

None.

Location and Space Needed

Players may prefer to do this indoors so that they will not feel too silly to be seen by others who are not participating. If they are a group of self-confident people, that will not matter.

Developmental Skills

Primary: verbal contact. Secondary: tactile contact, pantomime, cooperation, skill and coordination, adaptability.

Cranes and Crows

Number of Players

5 to 50+.

When to Play the Game

Best played in the middle of a session, but it could lead off or end it, too.

Description of Game

Are you a crow or a crane? To be honest, it does not matter, because whichever one you are, you may soon become the other. Or one or some of them will join you.

Set up boundaries for a rectangle wide enough to accommodate all players along a middle line (it can be invisible between two markers).

Divide the group into two lines, with the players in each line side by side and facing one another over the middle line two arms' lengths apart. Each group of players has a safety line about 30 feet (9 meters) behind it, parallel to the middle line. One line of players are the cranes and the other the crows.

The games leader stands at one end of the lines and shouts the name of one of the lines: *crows*, *cranes*, or any word beginning with a *c* or *cr*, such as *chrome*, *cranium*, *cronies*, *crater*. The reason for using other words that sound like but are not *crows* or *cranes* is to get players to listen carefully. It is fun to fake them out!

Only when a team's name is called does it chase the other line and try to tag them before they run back to reach their safety line, about 30 feet in the back of them, depending on the age and ability of the group. That is, the younger or more able, the farther the line. Anyone caught joins the other team, changing from a crane to a crow or vice versa. The teams then reform their lines in the middle and repeat the process.

Players who were crows but are now cranes must remember this fact. And it does not matter. Many players get confused no matter what. That is part of the fun.

Safety Instructions

Many people get very confused about whether they are coming or going, and although that is part of the fun, it sometimes means that they are running into other players. Just remind players to take care of one another.

Age Level

All. For younger players, you may need to select simpler words. This is a good game for them to learn to distinguish spoken sounds.

Equipment Needed

Boundary markers such as ropes, cones, or something similar, especially for younger players. Older players are more able to get by with abstract ideas like a safety line "even with that tree over there."

Location and Space Needed

Indoors or out. A fairly large open space without obstacles.

Developmental Skills

Primary: running, adaptability, tactile contact, reaction. Secondary: self-control, visual ability, speed.

Group Juggle

Number of Players

5 to 35. For more than 20 players, start two or more groups.

When to Play the Game

Not a good starting game. Any time in the middle of a games session.

Description of Game

Juggling as an individual is quite a challenge, and in pairs it requires much concentration. Juggling as a group (the way described here, anyway) requires attention but is actually easier.

Arrange the group into a circle. Have everyone put their hands in front of them as if to catch a ball. Throw a foam ball to someone in the circle, and ask her to throw it to someone else. Ask players to remember who threw the ball to them and whom they throw the ball to. Repeat this instruction now and then. After throwing the ball, the person who threw it lowers her hands, and the person throwing can throw only to someone who has his hands up. After the last person who had his hands up receives the ball, he throws it to the one who first threw it, thus completing a pattern including everyone. Do it one more time, a little faster, just for practice.

You can do many things to make this game more interesting. For instance, add another ball to the pattern. After the group masters that, add another, and then another. See how many balls the group can manage while being careful to avoid crashing balls together. We can also reverse the pattern. Or have some balls going forward and some backward. Or, after throwing a ball to a person, have the thrower jog over to take the receiver's place in the circle. Meanwhile, the receiver throws the ball to the next person and does the same. Any time a ball drops, just pick it up and throw it again.

If the group can do all these things, the biggest challenge is to have them move continuously around spontaneously in a given area and keep the pattern going. Calling out the name of the person that you are throwing to is very helpful. It may look like anarchy, but it actually can be very orderly. And definitely fun.

Safety Instructions

When players start moving, remind them to be careful about not crashing into one another.

Age Level

5 years and older. With younger players, you may need to have them roll the balls and use only one ball.

Equipment Needed

3 to 5 foam balls.

Location and Space Needed

Indoors or out. Only enough room for a circle of players, except

for the last suggestion, moving spontaneously, which needs a bit more space.

Developmental Skills

Primary: self-control, throwing and catching, adaptability, cooperation, visual ability, skillfulness and coordination. Secondary: verbal contact, running.

I Have a Friend...

Number of Players

5 to 50+.

When to Play the Game

Any time: beginning, middle, or even at the end.

Description of Game

Everyone likes to have a friend. We are, after all, a society of people. Just think—you can potentially have a whole circle of friends in this game!

Get the group in a circle, and use one less chair (or place marker) than the number of people playing. One person standing in the middle of the circle says, for example, "I have a friend who wears tennis shoes." People wearing tennis shoes get up and switch chairs or places with one another. The person in the middle tries to get a place, too. One person who is left standing (who has no chair or place marker) is the next leader. Here are some other examples that the person in the middle might say: I have a friend who plays basketball, or has two brothers, or has a birthday in July.

Keep some rules in mind: You cannot go back to the same chair or marker you just had, and you cannot go to the chair or marker next to you, unless it is the last place left open. You may not end up close friends with everyone in this game, but everyone will have better feelings toward one another.

Safety Instructions

There is no fighting or pushing to get a place—the first one there gets it. When many people are changing places, they need to remain aware of one another. If they get a little rough, you can start by reminding them playfully, "Remember, it *is* a game." If that doesn't help, ask the group how to keep it safe. If that doesn't work, suggest some means of locomotion that slows players down. If none of this works, you can always switch to another game.

Age Level

All.

Equipment Needed

Chairs, or place markers such as poly spots or carpet squares.

Location and Space Needed

Indoors or out. Room for a circle of players to spread out without obstruction in the middle of the circle.

Developmental Skills

Primary: tactile contact, self-control, speed, visual ability. Secondary: verbal contact, reaction, running, adaptability.

I Sit in the Grass With My Friend...

Number of Players

10 to 35. For more players, split the group after demonstrating.

When to Play the Game

A good game to start with or do near the beginning because it is funny, nobody is embarrassed, there's little physical contact, and you can learn the names of the other players. However, it is fun to do any time.

Description of Game

A great fun way to learn names is with a game I first came across in Germany. It is hectic and confusing at times, and people are bound to mess up spectacularly. In other words, it's a lot of fun. Now, I know you might be thinking, *But we already know everybody's name.* It doesn't matter. It just means the game will go a little faster, which makes it more fun, especially when someone inevitably does the wrong thing. Everyone cracks up!

We set up by arranging chairs or place markers in a circle with one more chair or marker than there are players. Then have each person say her name in turn going around the circle. After a demonstration, the game begins by having the two people who are on either side of the empty chair race to sit in it. The one who wins says, "I sit." The person who had been seated next to the winner moves back next to him while saying, "In the grass."

Finally, the person who had been seated next to the person who said, "In the grass," scoots into the empty chair or space next to him while saying, "With my friend . . ." and naming or pointing to someone in the group. (Note: If a person is pointed at, that person says her name so that the one who pointed at her, as well as the group, can learn her name.) The person named or pointed to moves to the empty chair, thereby leaving behind a new empty chair, which starts the game all over with a new race by the players on either side of that chair to be the first to move to the empty chair and say, "I sit." After a while, when the players get the idea of the game, ask them to see if they can speed up. This means players have to make quick decisions, and when they are caught just sitting, it is hilarious for the player and everyone else. Believe it or not, it's much easier to do this than to explain it!

Safety Instructions

If you see that the game is getting too rough, make a new rule that the first one to get his hand on the chair gets to sit on it. This can help prevent injury to fellow players and damage to the chairs. I used to say that this is particularly true for very young or very old players, but in truth, it applies to all ages.

Age Level

For younger players the game may need to be simplified: Just have one person move and say, "I sit in the grass with my friend . . ." rather than three people. To make sure everyone is involved, ask players to only name someone who has not been named.

Equipment Needed

Chairs, poly spots, carpet squares, or some other place markers.

Location and Space Needed

For outdoors, place markers work better than chairs. Enough space is needed to hold a circle of players with nothing in the middle.

Developmental Skills

Primary: self-control, reaction. Secondary: verbal contact, visual ability, problem solving, cooperation, adaptability, skillfulness and coordination, endurance, jumping.

In the Manner of the Adverb

Number of Players

5 to 50+.

When to Play the Game

Recommended for the middle of a games session.

Description of Game

Okay, raise your hand if you know what an adverb is. Uh-huh. Thought so. Very few. I must admit I was a bit hazy about what an adverb was until I played this game. Now I will never forget.

When starting, after you explain the game, several players—the guessers—go out of earshot to choose several verbs while the group chooses an adverb (a word describing a verb, like *quickly*, as in *run quickly*). The guessers return and give a verb that the group must do in the manner of the adverb that they have chosen. For instance, if the guessers' word is *dance*, and the group has chosen *slowly* as the adverb, then the group must dance slowly.

Guessers guess the adverb based on what they see. If wrong, guessers give another verb, for example, *swim*, and try again. After the group gets the idea, have the group choose both an easy and a hard adverb so that the guessers have a taste of success and a challenge. We do the easy one first. I doubt that players will ever forget what an adverb is after playing this game.

Safety Instructions

If the guessers are really stumped, give them the first letter of the adverb, and later, if necessary, the second letter, and more as needed.

Age Level

8 years and older. The game can be done with younger players in several ways. One is to name several adverbs beforehand, one of which will be used. Another is to use simple verbs instead of adverbs to act out for the guessers.

Equipment Needed

None.

Location and Space Needed

Indoors or out. Room for players to act out adverbs. The space need not be completely clear.

Developmental Skills

Primary: problem solving, self-control, creativity, pantomime, visual ability.
Secondary: verbal contact, adaptability, skillfulness and coordination, spontaneity, running, jumping, crawling, leaning on, balance.

La Ba Doo

Number of Players

5 to 50+.

When to Play the Game

In the middle or toward the end of a session. A good preliminary trust activity because it involves a fair amount of touching. It is a good game to use to end the session because all the players are focused together.

Description of Game

You can't dance? No matter. In the La Ba Doo dance, no one will notice. Everyone will be occupied with the extraordinary things they are doing.

First, form a fairly close circle facing in. A song and very simple dance are the main parts of this game. Our dance pattern is a simple side step, step together, and repeat in time to the song. The melody is the same as "Mary Had A Little Lamb." No real singing or dancing skills are necessary; just stay with the group as much as possible. Here are the words to the song:

Now we do the La Ba Doo,

La Ba Doo, La Ba Doo.

Now we do the La Ba Doo,

La Ba, La Ba, Doo. Hey!

The steps are done in time to the song, and the "Hey!" is accompanied by a vigorous final stomp of the foot. Then a second chorus is repeated going in the opposite direction. After the group does the La Ba Doo song and dance, you might ask them if they have done the La Ba Doo dance. After they have answered, "Yes!" ask if they have done the La Ba Doo dance with hands on a neighbor's shoulders ("No!"). Then proceed to do it.

Next, ask if they've done the dance with a finger on a neighbor's ear ("No!"). Then do it. Here are some other suggestions: hands on belly, finger on nose, hands on knees, and fingers on toes.

After doing all these, especially after finishing with "fingers on toes," you can ask the group if they have done the La Ba Doo dance in each way. After asking about the last one ("Have you done the La Ba Doo dance with fingers on toes?" "Yes!"), the group cannot imagine what could be next. You can then end by saying something like "Congratulations! We're finished." No doubt you will receive a cheer.

Safety Instructions

Tell people not to stress themselves, especially for touching the toes. Ask them to simply do the best they can, especially if they have back trouble.

Age Level

All.

Equipment Needed

None.

Location and Space Needed

Enough room for a fairly large circle.

Developmental Skills

Primary: tactile contact, self-control. Secondary: cooperation, verbal contact, adaptability, skillfulness and coordination, balance.

Lemonade 💿

Number of Players

5 to 50+.

When to Play the Game

A good game any time, but probably better in the middle of a session because it takes a while to set up. Can also be a good game to close with.

Description of Game

People love to keep playing this game on and on. It can keep going because players keep changing sides back and forth, so no one loses. It might never end.

Two teams form and huddle at their safety lines, which are 30 feet (9 meters) apart and parallel: The playing field is shaped like a square or rectangle. Each team chooses a place they are all from—it can be anywhere in the universe—and a job or trade that they can mime, which is not necessarily connected to the place. The teams stand facing each other on their safety lines.

The group that starts first takes a step toward the other team and then says, "Here we come!" The second team takes a step toward the middle while returning the refrain "Where are you from?" While continuing to alternate taking steps toward one another for each spoken phrase, the groups in turn say this to one another:

First: Group answers where they are from (for instance, "Pluto").

Second: "What's your trade?"

First: "Lemonade!" (Note: They don't tell their actual trade.)

Second: "Show us if you're not afraid!"

(Note: The two lines of players should be able to reach out and touch hands by now. Have them move closer together if they can't.) At this point the

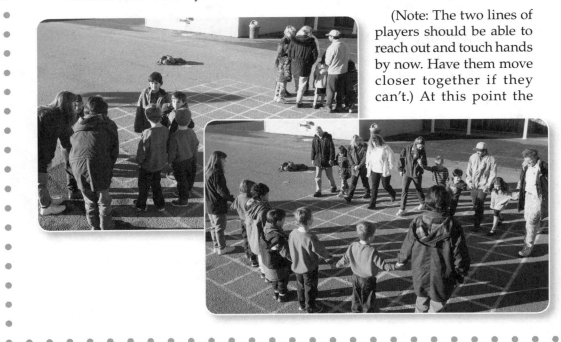

first group mimes their trade (job), while the second group tries to guess what it is. When even one person from the second team guesses correctly, the first team turns and runs back to their safety line. The second team tries to tag them before the first reach their line. If they reach it without being tagged, they are safe, but if they are tagged, they must join the other team.

Then, the second team has a turn, starting from their safety line. If they've caught anyone, their new team tells them where they're from and their trade. After that, both groups repeat the process. Who knows, with players moving back and forth, they might learn something about recycling.

Safety Instructions

Remind players to be careful about crashing into one another as they run; players often run the wrong way right into their pursuers.

Age Level

All. You may need to help preschool and primary school players identify jobs that the other team can guess. Elderly people can play this game at a slower pace, such as walking.

Equipment Needed

Something to create two lines, such as ropes or cones, though existing landmarks such as a tree or bush can be used, if necessary, to mark an invisible line.

Location and Space Needed

A space that is at least 30 feet (9 meters) wide and clear of obstacles. With younger children, you may want to expand the boundaries to give them more of a chance to burn up excess energy; conversely, you may want to shrink the boundaries for older people.

Developmental Skills

Primary: creativity, pantomime, visual ability, reaction, speed, running, problem solving, self-control. Secondary: verbal contact, tactile contact, adaptability, spontaneity.

Line Up

Number of Players

10 to 50.

When to Play the Game

Any time is fine. It could be a game to open with since it is nonthreatening and brings the group together. Usually the playing time is pretty brief.

Description of Game

"Get in a circle." That is mostly what you hear when playing New Games. It gets to be a bit repetitive. Here is a game to bring a little comic relief.

Have the group form a square, facing inward, with approximately the same number of players in each line. This in itself is a reason to do the game, since it is one of the only games that uses this shape. The leader gets in the middle, facing one of the lines. One side of the square is on his right side, one on his left, and one is in back of him. All players must take note of where they are in relation to the person in the middle *and* where they are in relation to one another in the line—specifically, who is on their left and right.

The middle player turns, and the lines must get back to the place they were (front, back, right, or left side) relative to the middle person and in the order they were originally in. When they have done that, they take one another's hands in their line, lift their arms in the air and shout, "Line up!" Each line wants to be first, of course. The player in the middle can go a quarter turn left or right, a half turn, three-quarter turn, or a full turn. This player can even go out from inside the square, and the lines must find their right places again. This game lasts only a few minutes, and what a relief to be in a shape other than a circle!

Safety Instructions

Players need to be careful not to hurt one another as they scramble to get to their new line. You may need to remind them or, if it is a recurring problem, change the locomotion to slow them down to a walk. Ask the players for suggestions.

Age Level

5 years and older. Young players may need acquaintance with the concept of a square.

Equipment Needed

None.

Location and Space Needed

Indoors or out. Enough open space for a square of players.

Developmental Skills

Primary: reaction, running, visual ability, self-control, cooperation. Secondary: speed, tactile contact, problem solving, adaptability.

Little Ernie

Number of Players

5 to 50+.

When to Play the Game

Any time is possible, but usually after the first game and before the last (for both it is important for you to create a good sense of group feeling).

Description of Game

Little Ernie has a family and a story, but the story does not exist yet. It is made up on the spot by your storyteller.

Start by making lines with five or six people in each line. Have each line stand at least 5 feet (1.5 meters) from its nearest neighbors. The object is to have enough room between each line so that every line can have a player running around it at the same time without any of the runners colliding. Each person in the line will get a role to play in the story about little Ernie and his family. The first person is little Ernie and the next people are members of his family, such as big sister, little brother, father, mother, grandparents, Spot the dog, Tiger the cat, and so on.

The leader then acts as storyteller. Later, we can change storytellers, if someone else wants that role. Every time one of the people in the line is mentioned in the story, he or she must run around his or her whole line, front and back. If they "all" are mentioned, they all go. It really gets to be fun if the characters act out the story as they run around. Generally, the story only lasts a few minutes, depending on the group's response. If the story is dragging, ask the storyteller to wind it up.

Safety Instructions

Make sure that the lines are not too close together so that circling family members do not bump into one another. If you notice collisions starting to happen, have the lines spread out a bit more.

Age Level

With the elderly or people with disabilities, change running to walking or as needed. With younger people who need more activity, you can have the runners go around the whole group (that is, all the lines).

Equipment Needed

None.

Location and Space Needed

If done indoors, a large, clear room is needed to hold lines of players.

Developmental Skills

Primary: self-control, reaction. Secondary: endurance, running, creativity, pantomime, spontaneity, verbal contact, speed.

Octopus

Number of Players

10 to 50+.

When to Play the Game

Good any time. Best sometime in the middle of a play session.

Description of Game

I played a game similar to this one in junior high at lunchtime recess. We played it almost every day, as I recall. I loved that game then. And I like it pretty well now, too, as do players.

Construct a fairly large square or rectangle, at least 30 square feet (9 square meters), and have the group (swimmers) get on one of the long sides, or shore. The opposite side is also a shore, with an "ocean" in between. There is an octopus (one player) in the middle of the ocean. When the octopus says, "Swim!" swimmers make swimming motions to cross the ocean while avoiding being caught by the octopus. The octopus has ink (foam ball) to capture swimmers by touching them with either a tag or throw. Once touched, a swimmer cannot move her legs anymore and her arms become tentacles of the octopus. Any swimmer she touches with her tentacles (arms) also becomes tentacles of the octopus.

If swimmers arrive safely on the distant shore, they stop for a breather until all the swimmers have made it over and wait for the octopus, who is in the center of the ocean again, to say, "Swim!" The last one caught can be the octopus for the next game, if he wishes.

Safety Instructions

This game is usually pretty safe, but overexuberant swimmers may need reminding that as they cross the ocean, they should not run into fellow swimmers or tentacles, and octopi need to be sure that their tentacle arms do not injure swimmers.

Age Level

5 years and older. It is possible to do with younger players if they are used to group activities or can be paired with an adult.

Equipment Needed

A foam ball, possibly two if you want to change the game a bit, and boundary markers such as cones, although boundaries can be improvised.

Location and Space Needed

Indoors or out, but in either case a fairly large space, about 30 by 30 feet (9 by 9 meters), or larger for more players or players in need of or wanting exercise.

Developmental Skills

Primary: running, speed, adaptability, visual ability, reaction, pantomime. Secondary: cooperation, tactile contact, problem solving, self-control, spontaneity, throwing and catching, verbal contact, skillfulness and coordination.

One Behind

Number of Players

5 to 50+.

When to Play the Game

Very good for stretching to start a session.

Description of Game

There are days when I seem to be not quite with it, one step behind things. In this game, you can be one step ahead if you are the leader. Otherwise, you will still be one step behind. Fortunately, so is everyone else except the leader.

The game is simplicity itself. The leader assembles the group so that the group can see her. Then she makes a simple movement and repeats it, such as lifting her right arm. Make sure to tell the group to do nothing. After five or so arm lifts, the leader makes a new movement, such as stretching her left hand to touch her toe. Now the group starts to do the first movement the leader made, the right arm lift. When the leader changes again, to walking in place, the group does the movement she just finished, the left arm stretch. This continues as the group does the movement the leader has just done—thus the name One Behind. Not to worry if you as a follower cannot remember the last movement—somebody else in the group will, and you can just copy that person.

Safety Instructions

Whether you or someone else is the leader, the movements must all be something everyone can do (no flips or forward rolls).

Age Level

5 years and older.

Equipment Needed

None.

Location and Space Needed

Indoors or out, with enough room for players to have a bit of movement within their own space.

Developmental Skills

Primary: cooperation, adaptability, self-control, visual ability. Secondary: problem solving, reaction, verbal contact, balance, creativity, spontaneity.

People to People

Number of Players

10 to 50+.

When to Play the Game

This is not usually a game to start with. Before playing this game, you should probably play some preliminary trust activities.

Description of Game

Talk about getting to know someone better! If you did not know someone beforehand, you will not easily forget that person after this.

Everyone gets a partner and creates a circle with enough room so that there is space between pairs. The leader is in the middle and begins by calling out two body parts that the partners must put together, such as elbow to knee. Both people can do this, although only one connection is necessary. After three to five calls, the leader calls, "People to people," at which point all the partners separate and run into the middle to find a new partner, including the leader.

The one person left without a partner becomes the new caller. If there is an even number of players, no problem—have two in the middle to start, and the last couple to find each other become the new callers. The game lasts for between 5 and 10 changes of leaders, whatever feels right. Although the connections are not cumulative to when the game is first introduced, it can be played that way after a round or two if the leader chooses to do so. Whenever you see someone with whom you have done finger to armpit, it is extremely likely to bring smiles to both of you.

Safety Instructions

To avoid any problems about which body parts are called, specify that it has to be something everyone could have, or simply agree beforehand to eliminate inappropriate areas such as lips, teeth, tongue, and so forth. Slow down the game for all if there are those who cannot run. You can have everyone walking, or walking heel to toe, while those who cannot move quickly or do any of these things can try to do the best they can. It is still fun. Adapt as needed.

Age Level

All. The very young can learn the different parts of their bodies this way.

Equipment Needed

None.

Location and Space Needed

A large space, about 30 by 30 feet (9 by 9 meters).

Developmental Skills

Primary: cooperation, tactile contact, self-control, speed. Secondary: problem solving, verbal contact, creativity, spontaneity, visual ability, skillfulness and coordination, reaction, running, leaning on, adaptability.

Scoot and Spell

Number of Players

10 to 35.

When to Play the Game

Good any time in the middle of a session.

Description of Game

Hey, here is a game where you learn something and have a blast doing it! Not only are players racing about frantically, they are also taking letters and trying to form words.

Divide the group into teams of three or four players and spread them in a circular pattern an equal distance from the middle, each with a marker to designate their base. In the middle there are cards with individual letters on them, turned face down. As a rule of thumb, for a group of 15, have at least four full alphabets with three sets of extra vowels.

The groups attempt to spell a word with at least four letters. To start, each group sends one person to get a letter. When she gets back, another group member gets a letter. Every member must go in turn. Each group keeps going until they get a word. I guarantee that you will never see players so excited about spelling words as in this game. And they are even getting a bit of exercise in the bargain.

Safety Instructions

Spread out the cards a little bit to avoid collisions of heads in the middle.

Age Level

5 years and older. For young players make it three- or even two-letter words. The point is to generate excitement around learning.

Equipment Needed

A minimum of about 150 small index cards. More is better for larger groups. (You'll need a marker for writing individual letters. Make sure that the letters do not bleed through. This must be done before presenting the game.)

Location and Space Needed

Indoors or outdoors, a space at least a 20 by 20 feet (6 by 6 meters).

Developmental Skills

Primary: cooperation, problem solving, verbal contact; self-control, creativity, spontaneity, running. Secondary: adaptability, visual ability, reaction, speed.

Ship Ahoy!

Number of Players

5 to 50+.

When to Play the Game

Any time.

Description of Game

Oh, for the life at sea, with the sky above and the sea below, stretching all the way to the horizon. For some, anyway, this is paradise, and as long as we are playing this game, we too can pretend to be on board.

One player is designated the caller for the rest of the players. A ship is defined with boundary markers; this could also be the walls of a room, if played indoors. The caller gives different instructions to the players, and the group must respond quickly. If a player is slow or gives the wrong response and is seen by the caller, that player changes places with the caller. Also, for certain calls players will need to run to one place or another on the ship. If the caller can catch someone before that person gets to his destination, the person caught becomes the new caller.

The caller can make these commands:

- "Ship ahoy!" is where all players put both hands up over their eyebrows as if to shade their eyes from the sun.
- "Scrub the decks!" means everyone must get on hands and knees and pretend to scrub the floor or ground.
- "Captain's coming!" causes players to stand up straight at attention and give a right-handed salute.
- "Forward" means all players must go to the place identified as the front of the ship. "Aft" means everyone goes to the back of the ship.
- "Port" means all players go to the left side of the ship.
- "Starboard" means all go to the right side of the ship.

Later, as players learn these commands, others can be added:

- "Man overboard" means everyone pretends to throw a life preserver to the person who went overboard.

- "Shipwreck" causes everyone to gather in groups of three, with one person in the middle and the other two holding hands around him to form a lifeboat.

As players become familiar with these commands, they can make up additional commands. If they can stand any more, that is.

If you get a leader who wants to stay the leader by not trying to catch anyone, switch leaders after five commands, and let a person be leader only once.

Safety Instructions

Remind players to look after one another when they have to run in a certain direction to avoid running into someone going the wrong direction. For commands where physical contact is required, make sure the group is comfortable with doing this, or find a way that is acceptable. (Instead of holding hands in shipwreck, for instance, players can take hold of a sleeve with their hands.)

Age Level

All. For younger players, start with few commands and add new commands as the group feels comfortable.

Equipment Needed

None necessary. Markers of some kind to designate forward, aft, and sides of the ship outside are useful, but can be improvised: lines on the pavement, trees, bushes, anything handy.

Location and Space Needed

Indoors or out, with room to allow players to move freely.

Developmental Skills

Primary: self-control, reaction, problem solving, pantomime, speed. Secondary: running, cooperation, verbal contact, tactile contact, creativity, visual ability, skillfulness and coordination, throwing, adaptability.

Snowball

Number of Players

5 to 50+.

When to Play the Game

Could be an opening game or in the middle of a session. Good to use when the group is starting out and the members are new or just getting to know each other.

Description of Game

It is September, the weather is hot, and I am proposing what—a snowball fight? Yes! Indeed. Who said you needed cold and snow? We can pretend for that part; all we need is scrap paper and a pen or pencil.

Divide the group into two teams. Make a middle line that no player can cross, dividing the groups, and sidelines that limit where you can throw. If you are indoors, this will divide the room in half. Each player writes his or her name on a piece of paper and wads it into a ball. Then, at a given signal, everyone throws their snowball across the line into the other team's territory. As other snowballs come into your territory, you can pick them up and throw them back. You may not cross over the center line. The idea of the game is to have the fewest snowballs on your side at the end. The game usually lasts about a minute, which does not sound like a long time unless you are playing. Then it seems like five minutes. As soon as a player picks up a snowball, they must throw it. No hoarding till the last moment.

To end, have every player get a snowball and open it to find the name inside, and ask everyone to find the person whose name is on the paper. This is particularly good when a group is new or just getting to know one another.

Didn't I tell you we could have a snowball fight in the heat?

Safety Instructions

Ask players to throw snowballs so that if they hit someone, it would not be in the face. Although there is not much chance of harm, getting hit in an open eye is not very pleasant. Also, make sure players do not cross the line to get snowballs, because they may end up bumping heads with players from the other team that way.

Age Level

5 years and older.

Equipment Needed

Paper and pencils or pens. Perhaps a rope or something to indicate the middle line and cones or markers for each group's side and back lines, although these all can be improvised.

Location and Space Needed

Indoors or outdoors. Size of space will depend on the number of players, but the absolute minimum space would be 20 by 20 feet (6 by 6 meters), maximum space 30 by 30 feet (9 by 9 meters).

Developmental Skills

Primary: throwing, catching, adaptability, self-control, visual ability, skillfulness and coordination, reaction. Secondary: verbal contact.

High Activity Games

Two games in this section, Base Tag and Germs and Doctors, were invented by participants at my workshops. Base Tag was created from the elements of running players, throwing, and baseball. What came out of that was a game exciting enough to stand on its own. There are players with balls trying to hit other players when they are off a base. If a player comes to a base and wants to get on, but it already has a player on it, the first player says, "Bye bye" or "Go," and the player on the base must go. It is fast paced, and for some reason it often comes as a surprise when someone claims your base. The group that invented the game got giddy playing it, and so did I! Now you have an opportunity to share this natural high.

Base Tag

Number of Players

10 to 50+.

When to Play the Game

If an active game is needed, this is a good choice. It could be a good starting game.

Description of Game

I have always thought that for a game named baseball, there were not that many bases. And only one ball. In Base Tag, we remedy that. There are other things that I prefer about Base Tag, namely, that everyone is always involved, there is a lot of movement—running and throwing—and most of all, there is continuous fun.

Spread bases throughout the desired play area, with approximately one base for every three players. Have a player with a foam ball (an "It") for every five players. If you are not It and are hit with a ball, you become It and take the ball to hit someone else who is not It. If you are on a base, you are safe and cannot be hit (and if you are hit, you are still not It). However, if someone comes up and wants the base, you must move and cannot immediately return to the same base. (The person wanting the base can say something to let the person on the base know that they must go, such as "Go" or "Bye-bye.") Remember, when someone is running and they need a base, they have no friends. So be prepared to move.

You have no foam balls? No problem. Then the Its must simply tag Not-Its.

Safety Instructions

As with any fast-moving game, there is always a danger of collisions, especially when the game is played in a confined space. Remind players to be alert and aware of each other so they can avoid crashes. Because players don't get running full steam, this is less of a problem.

Age Level

All. Like almost all games in this book, minimum age is 4.

Equipment Needed

A base (carpet square, poly spot, marker) for every three players and a ball for every five.

Location and Space Needed

Indoors or out. The game can be played in a small space like a classroom or on a large one, like a football field. If space is very limited, one possibility is to have half the group play while the other watches. Or maybe all can play if you change from running to a fast walk (the front foot must be down before the back foot can be picked up).

Developmental Skills

Primary: throwing and catching, running, speed, visual ability. Secondary: verbal contact, cooperation, adaptability, self-control, reaction, endurance, jumping.

Blob

Number of Players

10 to 50+.

When to Play the Game

This game could be played any time, except after another very active game.

Description of Game

The name of this game was derived from the movie *The Blob*. In playing the game, you can pretend that a UFO has landed in your town and, just like in the movie, some kind of gooey alien has started catching people and turning them into blobs. And, also like in the movie, when a blob gets to be a certain size, it splits into two blobs.

In this game, however, the human race loses as everyone becomes a blob. Oh, well.

What actually happens in the game is that, after defining the play area, you somehow find someone to be your initial blob. Arbitrariness is fine, as long as the person agrees to be the blob. Then that person must, within the defined boundaries, catch another person by tagging them. They then link by holding hands

and can catch someone only while being linked. When they catch someone, the third person links with them as well. Only the outside hand on either end of the blob can tag players. However, when a fourth person is caught, something special happens: mitosis! For nonbiologists, it means the blob divides in two. Now two blobs stalk humans. Each time there are four in a blob, they can divide again. After a while, there is nowhere a poor human can go to escape. What fun!

Safety Instructions

Since everyone is racing madly about, remind players to be aware of each other to avoid crashing into one another. Although this applies a lot to younger players, teens and even adults need to be aware of what they are doing, too. And since they are bigger, they can do more damage when they do smack into someone else. As in any tag game, if tags become too rough, it may need to be pointed out that a tag is a touch, not a hit.

Age Level

6 on up. Younger players might understand, but it is not a given. Once children start working in groups, they can usually grasp the idea. For senior citizens, have everyone slow down or walk if running is too strenuous.

Equipment Needed

None. Cones or some other boundary markers are useful but not necessary.

Location and Space Needed

Usually, in a large space whether in or outdoors. With elderly or people who are less mobile, a small space is fine. While a large space is useful, it is not absolutely necessary. For small spaces, change the manner of moving to slow players down. For instance, have everyone walk heel to toe.

Developmental Skills

Primary: cooperation, verbal contact, tactile contact, self-control, visual ability, reaction, speed, running. Secondary: adaptability, problem solving, spontaneity, pantomime, endurance, balance.

Borrow It

Number of Players

10 to 50+.

When to Play the Game

Could be any time, but probably better sometime in the middle.

Description of Game

Thieving is wrong, but it is not stealing if you are welcomed by your neighbors to borrow something. Sometimes it happens that neighbors are so friendly that you do not even have to ask—you just pop into their house and borrow almost anything. You know they will do the same and it will all balance out in the end. Okay, you ask, what planet are you from? I actually know people and places where this is done. Really. Not in the city. You can do the same, at least in this game.

Divide the group into smaller groups of four (or some number near that, as long as all the groups are fairly close in numbers). Have each group choose four or five items (such as Frisbees, balls, stuffed animals) plus a base to put them on (or in—hula hoops are great for the base). Have the groups spread out in a circle at least 10 feet (3 meters) apart from one another; the ideal situation is to have all groups an equal distance from one another. After placing the items on their base or in their hoop, have all players put one foot on their base before starting.

When everyone is ready, count to three to start, after which every player will go to the bases of another group and "borrow" an object to bring back to their own base. A player can take no more than one object at a time, must place it on or in their base, not throw it in, and may not throw it to another player on their team. No player can guard their base or obstruct players from other teams—they can only get objects from other teams' bases. The game lasts only a minute—longer only if your players have enough energy; it's exhausting! Whichever group has the most objects wins—but no time to gloat; it's time to

redistribute the objects and do it again, or go on to another game! So now that you have done the game, you will not mind my coming into your house to borrow things, right?

Safety Instructions

The main concern is players bumping into other players as they rush to and fro, especially when they get an object and turn to run before looking to see if someone is there. The other concern is that some players will try to guard their base, banging into other players in the process. Remind players not to do it, and if that does not work, ask them to stop doing that or leave the game.

Age Level

5 years and older. For younger players, you can have shorter distances.

Equipment Needed

Carpet squares or some other item, such as hula hoops, for bases, and enough objects so that each team has four or five.

Location and Space Needed

Outdoors is better, but indoors works. A minimum of 20 by 20 feet (6 by 6 meters) is needed indoors, although larger is better.

Developmental Skills

Primary: running, self-control, adaptability, visual ability. Secondary: problem solving, tactile contact, cooperation, spontaneity, skillfulness and coordination, endurance.

Cat and Mice 💿

Number of Players

10 to 50.

When to Play the Game

A game to do after other preliminary trust games have been done by the group and some good feelings have been generated, since this is a very vigorous and physical game. This is a great game for a restless group needing movement and needing to get some gentle aggression out.

Description of Game

Cat and mice? Uh-oh, the mice might be devoured. But no. Actually the cat in this game is a vegetarian (picture that!) and an indoctrinator. Kitty not only does not eat mousy but also convinces captured mice to help catch other mice till all are caught.

We start with a cat in the middle of a rectangular field facing a line of mice on one wide side of a rectangle, which is at least 30 feet wide and long enough to comfortably fit all mice. Cat and mice are at least 15 feet (4.5 meters) apart. When the cat meows or says, "Go," the mice must cross the playing area to the other side to a boundary at least 15 feet in back of the cat to be safe. They wait there for the next signal to go. Meanwhile, the cat catches as many mice as possible merely by tagging them, which transforms them into mousetraps. They join the cat in the middle to start each round. Any mice who run out of the boundaries are automatically caught.

Once a player becomes a mousetrap, he or she can move about trying to catch and hold mice until the cat tags the mouse and transforms her or him, too. If the cat takes no notice, the mousetrap can yell, "Cat, cat," for attention. When a mouse is caught by a mousetrap, it can try to get away, but neither the mouse

nor the mousetrap can use so much force that they hurt the other. Eventually all the mice are caught, or maybe there is one left, who is invited to become the cat for the next round of the game. And no dead mice.

Safety Instructions

While this game is a lot of fun, it has the potential for overly rough action. If you notice players becoming too rough, stop the game and remind everyone that it is no fun if someone gets hurt. You can also let players know that they can say, "Stop!" any time they feel they are being hurt, and all the other players must agree to stop.

Another way to approach the problem is to tell the players that the game is getting too rough and ask for solutions to make it safe for all. Usually they come up with imaginative ideas, and this way they have ownership of the solution, which means they are more likely to follow it. As a last resort, you can suggest something to slow the game down, such as walking or hopping rather than running. The main thing is to keep the game safe for all.

Age Level

All. Players between the ages of 10 and 20 are most prone to be rough, so be especially aware of how they are playing.

Equipment Needed

Existing lines on a field, or boundary markers such as cones, Frisbees, tapes, or ropes are helpful, but these can be improvised (such as shoes or rucksacks).

Location and Space Needed

If done indoors, a large area is needed, and preferably one that is soft, perhaps with mats. If done outdoors, grass or other soft surfaces are best.

Developmental Skills

Primary: tactile contact, adaptability, running, strength, cooperation, self-control. Secondary: endurance, visual ability, skillfulness and coordination, speed.

Clothespin Tag

Number of Players

5 to 50+.

When to Play the Game

Although this could be a game to open or close with, it is probably best left for the middle of a session.

Description of Game

I remember once in Germany dressing up like a punk with my hair in spikes for a party. The effect was continued with clothespins attached to parts of my head where there was no hair—ears, cheeks, lips and chin. It is not something I would recommend for a long time (5 minutes or so), but it did make for a dramatic entrance to the party. The point is to show that clothespins can be used for more than hanging up clothes. For instance, the game of Clothespin Tag.

It does not take a physicist to figure out that to play this game you need clothespins, ideally enough so that every player can get three, but make this fewer if not. Have them attach the pins on their sleeves at the shoulder level. If they do not have sleeves, they could put the pins on the sides of their shirts at hip level. Do not allow them to clip pins to the front or back of their shirts, trousers, or skirts. If they do so, when other players try to get the pins, it can get way too personal, even if unintentionally. The idea is that once you start, get as many clothespins from other players as possible.

Each time a pin is obtained, the person getting it has three seconds to put it on their sleeve; they will count out loud "One, two, three." During this time, no one can take one of their pins, but once they are finished, they are fair game once again.

Before starting, define some boundaries, not too big a space, because we want people to be able to get to each other easily, but large enough so that everyone can move around comfortably. Point out that players may not guard their pins by putting their hands over them or by pushing other players' hands away. All a player can do is move away. This game does not last long, about a minute or so, after which everyone will be a bit pooped. Just for fun, see how many pins different players got. However, if this gets too competitive, skip this step in succeeding times played. And, no, players are not allowed to attach clothespins to their skin—this isn't a punk party!

Clothespin Tag

Safety Instructions

The thing that could keep this game from being fun is deliberate inappropriate touching, so the placement of the clothespins is important. Put the pins where this will not be a problem, as suggested, on the shoulder or hip.

Age Level

5 years and older.

Equipment Needed

Clothespins (now there's a surprise!).

Location and Space Needed

Indoors or out, with at least a space at least 20 by 20 feet (6 by 6 meters), and bigger for a larger group.

Developmental Skills

Primary: tactile contact, adaptability, self-control, visual ability, skillfulness and coordination, reaction, speed, running. Secondary: problem solving, verbal contact, endurance, leaning on.

Elbow Tag 🔘

Number of Players

10 to 35 players; divide the group and make two games for more players.

When to Play the Game

A great game to do any time. Because it does involve touching, it might not be best to start with, but is a good preliminary trust game.

Description of Game

Players on the run in this game will grab anyone to keep from getting caught, even people they might not normally relate to at all. So it is a good mixer, breaking down barriers between players.

Everyone takes a partner and links together at the elbow; use one threesome if there is an odd number of players. The leader and his or her partner unlink and begin the game by having a round of tag. As usual, if the person who is It succeeds in touching the other, they reverse roles: The runner becomes It, and the It becomes the runner. The other partners remain linked and stationary. If the person being chased wants to quit running, or is about to be caught, he can grab onto the elbow of anyone who is linked to someone else, and shout, "Go!"

This means the person on the other end of what has become a threesome must let go of her former partner's elbow because she is now the new person being chased. Other players can cheer her on (and remind her of what she must do) by also saying, "Go" to keep the game going, and to sustain their interest.

After a while, introduce the idea that if the person who is It becomes tired, he may also grab any elbow of a linked pair, passing on his role of It to the end person of this new threesome.

When the chaser does this, he shouts, "You're It!" so the person leaving the threesome knows which role she is. Again, other players are encouraged to do this as well. You'll be surprised how eager players are to grab an elbow when they need one, no matter whom it belongs to!

Safety Instructions

Having the chaser be able to take an elbow saves them from the embarrassment of not being able to catch someone. You can introduce this possibility sooner than you planned if you see someone is having trouble. Also, this is a fast-paced game; sometimes players get confused and may run into each other, or crash into pairs. If you see that people are running recklessly, have players slow down or walk, or have the group come up with a solution that is fun.

Age Level

8 years and older. Younger players might find it difficult to understand. If you do it with this age, don't introduce the part where the It can change until they've really got it, maybe not even in the first time using the game. If someone can't catch anyone, stop the game and ask who would now like to be It.

Equipment Needed

None.

Location and Space Needed

A cleared area with enough room to do some running.

Developmental Skills

Primary: reaction, adaptability, speed, tactile contact, self-control, visual ability.
Secondary: spontaneity, running, verbal contact.

Everybody Bats

Number of Players

10 to 35, best with numbers in the middle of that range.

When to Play the Game

The middle of a session is best, but it could be played any time, or even on its own.

Description of Game

The bad part about baseball is waiting. Waiting to bat, waiting for the ball to come to you in the field, or waiting to be involved in a play. In this game, every player gets to bat each time their team is batting, and every player in the field takes part in every play.

To begin, form two teams. Although ability level matters little, you can ask players to partner up with someone about their own ability level, and then have the partners split up to make the teams. The team batting sends up a batter—it does not matter who, since everyone will get a turn—who hits a ball gently pitched by someone from the opposing team. No matter where a struck ball goes—forward, sideways, or backward—the batter starts to run around his or her team. Each cycle around his or her team is a run, which the whole team counts out loud. Naturally, the closer together teammates get, the less distance the batter needs to run.

Meanwhile, it does not matter who has gotten the ball on the fielding team. The rest of the team will form a line behind that person, facing the same direction. The ball is passed back from teammate to teammate in the line, first between the legs and then the next one over the head, with that pattern repeating until the ball reaches the end of the line. When that happens, the last player in line holds the ball in the air and shouts, "Done!"

However many times the batter has circled the team while the fielded ball was being passed down the line is the number of runs he has made for the team.

Every player on the batting team takes a turn, and the total runs of all the batters are added for the team's score. Then the opposing team has a similar turn at bat. Having watched many a baseball game over the years, I have to say I find this much more exciting. It definitely has more activity.

Safety Instructions

Using a soft large ball ensures that no one is injured by a batted ball. High-bounce foam balls are great for this.

Age Level

5 years and older. Using a large ball, even a beach ball, is especially important for younger players.

Equipment Needed

A bat and a large soft ball, like a high-bounce foam ball and one base.

Location and Space Needed

Indoors or out in a large space. Outdoors is best, but a gym or very large room would work.

Developmental Skills

Primary: cooperation, self-control, reaction, running, speed, throwing and catching. Secondary: verbal contact, tactile contact, adaptability, visual ability, skill-fulness and coordination.

Everybody's It 💿

Number of Players

5 to 50+.

When to Play the Game

A great game to start with, or for any time. Great for a group needing movement, and a good preliminary trust activity because it involves minimal nonthreatening touching.

Description of Game

Whoever heard of a tag game where everyone was it? I did, for one. As unlikely as it sounds, it is easy to involve all players in this easy to play game.

   Yes, this *is* a tag game (the one who is It attempts to tag someone else to make him or her It) where everybody is It and can tag everyone else. However, once a person is tagged, she or he must freeze until the end of the game, which in fact comes quickly. However, if someone who is not frozen comes too near a frozen person, the one who is frozen can temporarily unfreeze an arm (and only an arm!) to reach out to tag and freeze the runner, before going back to being frozen him- or herself. The game goes until everyone is frozen, or just one is left.

A variation of this is Hospital Tag. In this game, you keep running the first and second times you are tagged, but you must hold the place you were tagged in both instances. The third time you are tagged, you are frozen, like for the game of Everybody's It, and once again you can temporarily unfreeze an arm to tag others who come too close.

Another variation that first-graders came up with at a school project I was involved with was that when you get tagged, you are frozen, and when you are tagged again by anyone, you are unfrozen, so the game can keep on going till everybody is tired.

Safety Instructions

As with most active games, when players are moving about quickly, there is danger of collisions. Remind players to be aware of where they are running to avoid crashes. If that doesn't work, try a fast walk (one foot must be down before the other is up) or some other way of moving.

Age Level

All.

Equipment Needed

Boundary markers such as cones, poly spots, Frisbees, or other such indicators are useful. Using existing boundaries such as trees, sidewalks, and bushes also works.

Location and Space Needed

A lot of clear space, minimum of 30 by 30 feet (9 by 9 meters).

Developmental Skills

Primary: running, speed, self-control, visual ability, reaction. Secondary: tactile contact, adaptability, spontaneity, endurance.

Fire Engine

Number of Players

5 to 50+.

When to Play the Game

In the middle of a session because it is a little silly for some to begin with. Could be a good game to end for children who have lots of energy left. A good first trust game because minimal touching with hands involved.

Description of Game

When I think of this game, the first image that comes to my mind is a group of 150 people in business attire madly racing back and forth as fire engines at a conference in Stockholm, Sweden. I couldn't contain my laughter at the irony of this hysterical scene. They were laughing, too.

First divide the group into lines of five or six players. Have them all make parallel lines pointing in the same direction. We pretend that there is a fire about 50 feet in front of the line, and we send the first person (or fire engine) in each line with their siren wailing (their vocalization) and light flashing (an arm flailing over the head) to put the fire out. When the engine (person) gets to the fire, she becomes a fire person holding a fire hose shooting water on the fire.

But it turns out to be a big fire, so the first engine goes back to the line to get a second engine from their own line, wailing and flailing the whole time. They both race off holding hands to put out the fire. This repeats until every person in each line has been fetched. By this time, with everyone rushing around holding hands and wailing like a siren, it is pure pandemonium. And, incidentally, a lot of fun. Ask the business people of Sweden.

Safety Instructions

As fire engines rush back and forth, they need to be careful not to crash into one another. A friendly reminder should take care of this, but if that is not enough, stop the game to make sure it's addressed. One solution is to move the groups farther apart. You can always ask the players for ideas on making it safer.

Age Level

All. For the elderly, running might be walking over a shorter distance. For antsy kids, the distance might be longer. Adapt as needed.

Equipment Needed

None. Any arbitrary object can be placed as the point where the "fire" is so that players know where to run.

Location and Space Needed

This can be played indoors, but usually it is best to have it in a gym or large activity room so that there is enough room to do it. For young players, you can lengthen the distance they run. With elderly players, you can make the distance shorter if necessary and not require running.

Developmental Skills

Primary: running, speed, jumping. Secondary: cooperation, tactile contact, pantomime, self-control, problem solving, skillfulness and coordination, endurance, creativity.

Germs and Doctors

Number of Players

10 to 50.

When to Play the Game

Any time an active game is called for.

Description of Game

There seem to be a lot of germs that we can catch today, and sometimes it seems like there is a shortage of doctors. While some people contend that we choose health or illness, we can represent the situation previously described with a game.

This is a form of tag where there is one player chosen to be a germ for every 5 players and a player chosen to be a doctor for every 10. When the game starts, germs attempt to tag people, who then collapse on the ground (a crouch will

suffice) and start calling out, "Doctor, doctor!" At this point, one of the players designated as a doctor can come to heal the sick with a touch.

Of course, doctors can get sick, too, and need a doctor. If all the doctors get infected, no one can be cured any longer. The game goes on until the germs and everyone get tired or all players are infected. This is also not a bad way to show what happens with real illness, diseases, and shortages of doctors.

Safety Instructions

Simply be aware of other players while moving about, since this is an active game.

Age Level

5 years and older.

Equipment Needed

Boundary markers are needed. These can be improvised if markers are not available.

Location and Space Needed

Indoors or out, with a fairly large space. If you have a small space, change locomotion to something slower than running.

Developmental Skills

Primary: running, speed, tactile contact, visual ability, adaptability, reaction.
Secondary: verbal contact, endurance, self-control, leaning on, cooperation.

Hug Tag

Number of Players

10 to 50+.

When to Play the Game

Sometime in the middle or close to the end of a session would be the best time to do this game, which usually means that people are more ready for close physical contact. A good preliminary trust builder.

Description of Game

People who might not be friendly or even know each other suddenly become very glad to see each other in Hug Tag when being pursued by an It. Who knows, they might even become friends!

If you had not guessed by now, this is a tag game, where a person who is It tries to catch and touch another player, making her It. So that everyone knows who is It, the It carries a ball or other object. When the It tags someone, the ball or object is passed on to the new It. Other players who are not It can avoid being tagged by either run-ning away or hugging another player. Hugs can last for only three seconds, however, and the It can count to three to make sure.

To make the game more interesting, more than one person can be It at the same time, thereby increasing the action. After a while, another challenge is to require more than two people in a hug—try three, four, more? Last, for the truly daring, players can be tagged in a hug if the It can touch the abdomen of any person in a hug. The result is closer hugs. This last measure is not for all groups, but if players are open to the idea, it can add a lot of fun. Any way you play this game, people seem to get closer.

Safety Instructions

This is a very active game with people running in all directions. Remind players that this is hug tag, not crash tag, and to look out for one another. If they are not careful, either suggest some way of making the game safe, such as skipping, or ask the group what can be done to make the game safe. As usual, make only one change at a time.

Modifications may have to be made for players who are a bit shy or reluctant to hug, such as putting hands on one another's shoulders, holding hands, or maybe even touching elbows. In extreme circumstances where players do not want to touch at all, having them hold on to a piece of clothing (like a sleeve) of another player might work.

Age Level

5 years and older.

Equipment Needed

Three to five balls or other objects that the Its can have. Other objects could include Frisbees, shirts, or whatever is available.

Location and Space Needed

Plenty of open space is needed, a minimum of 30 by 30 feet (9 by 9 meters).

Developmental Skills

Primary: reaction, running, speed, endurance. Secondary: trust, visual ability, cooperation, adaptability, self-control, spontaneity.

Loose Caboose

Number of Players

10 to 50+ (at least three trains and one caboose needed).

When to Play the Game

In the middle or at the end of a games session.

Description of Game

The caboose has gone the way of many things from the past. It is but a memory to some and not even that to most. Here is a chance to relive the memory of the long-gone caboose, which was a special car at the end of a train. (Oh, how soon they forget!)

Have the participants get into groups of three. If there are a few left over, they will become loose cabooses. If everyone is in a group of three, ask one group to become the loose cabooses. Make sure there is a caboose for every two or three trains. Each group of three will form a train, with one person behind another. The person behind puts his hands on the waist of the person in front.

On the command of "Start," the trains chug around the area and the cabooses quickly seek a train to join. This means that they attach to the last person in the train by taking hold of the person's waist. When they do so, they yell, "Go!" This is the signal for the engine, or the first person in the train to disconnect, thereby becoming a loose caboose. The trains move to keep this from happening, trying to dodge the cabooses. This, of course, should all be done within a defined area, or you may find trains headed for destinations unknown. The game goes on until players start to tire, about a few minutes. And think of all we've done for the history of trains!

Safety Instructions

All players need to remain aware of one another—when moving to avoid a caboose, the train may be crashing into another train, possibly hurting play-

Loose Caboose

ers. If it becomes a problem, slow down the locomotion of the players, by walking, for instance. If players are sensitive about having someone's hands on their waist, have players hold on to each other's shoulders.

Age Level

8 years and older.

Equipment Needed

Boundary markers, possibly, but these can be improvised. It's important to clearly define the playing area.

Location and Space Needed

Indoors or out. A large clear space is best—minimum of 30 by 30 feet (9 by 9 meters). It is advisable to set boundaries. Pavement is not the best surface for this game, although it is possible if the group does not get rough.

Developmental Skills

Primary: cooperation, tactile contact, running, self-control, reaction. Secondary: problem solving, verbal contact, adaptability, pantomime, visual ability, speed, endurance, leaning on.

Monarch

Number of Players

5 to 50+.

When to Play the Game

Any time.

Description of Game

Having worked in Europe a lot in the past, I became fairly familiar with the idea of a monarch—a king or queen. They do not rule anymore, of course, but have only a ceremonial significance. That all changes in the game Monarch! The queen or king rules!

One person starts as the monarch. She has a foam ball that she can throw to hit another player and get that player to become a monarch, too. The first person can run with the ball, but once she hits someone with it, no one who is a monarch can move while holding the ball. After that, the monarchs must either pass the ball or throw it at a nonmonarch as soon as they catch it, using teamwork to capture others. It is useful to give monarchs a signal to identify one another: the person with the ball can yell, "Monarch!" and all those who are monarchs raise their arms. Monarchs without the ball can move about freely, getting near those who have not been caught to catch a pass and hit them more easily.

The game goes until all players are captured. It is important to have boundaries, the size of which will depend on the group (large for active children, small for the aged). This was the most popular game at the research project I did at a Sheffield school. I introduced the game recently, and someone thought *monarch* meant the butterfly. It could. You can invent a story to go with it to introduce the game.

Safety Instructions

Monarchs must hit the other players below the knees to capture them. Though the foam balls are soft, a shot to the head is still something that all can do without. By making the target area below the knees, it's much less likely someone will get hit in the head. If someone is hit above the knee, they are not caught.

Age Level

8 years and older.

Equipment Needed

One or two foam balls—high-bounce variety is the best, and something to mark the boundaries with, though this can be improvised.

Location and Space Needed

Indoors or out. A large space is usually required, 30 by 30 feet (9 by 9 meters) minimum for a small group, even if the locomotion is changed to walking. A larger space is better for a large group.

Developmental Skills

Primary: cooperation, verbal contact, visual ability, throwing and catching, adaptability, self-control, reaction, running, endurance. Secondary: problem solving, spontaneity, speed, skillfulness and coordination, jumping.

Partner Tag

Number of Players

10 to 50+.

When to Play the Game

Any time. Not most likely first or last, but could be.

Description of Game

Did you ever play a game of tag where there was only one It and that person could not catch anyone? It was pretty embarrassing for them and you may have felt embarrassed for them, too. You may have even let them catch you so that they would not feel so bad. That will never happen with this game. For one thing, the focus of attention is only between you and your partner. Nobody notices how well or badly anybody else is doing, and everybody is laughing so hard that they do not care anyway.

As you may have surmised, everyone needs to get a partner. If someone is left over, there can be one group of three. This is a tag game, but only with your partners. The game is played in a fairly small area so that it is a little bit crowded, and therefore players do not run but "fast walk," or have the front foot down before the other can be lifted, to keep players safe. Each set of partners decides who will be It, then that person counts to 5 to give the partner a chance to get away. If anyone bumps into anyone else, they must stop, shake hands, and both say to each other, "This will never happen again." When the It catches their partner, the partner who is now It counts to five before pursuing. This game does not last all that long—only a minute or two—because by then everyone is huffing and puffing even though no one is running. And did I mention that no one got embarrassed? You know I did.

Safety Instructions

Make sure that people are not running—that is unsafe in a confined area with everyone moving helter-skelter. Also, keep an eye out to see that people are stopping to shake hands when they bump. The game can easily get out of hand if you don't do this. Because shaking hands slows them down, they will try harder to avoid bumping into others. Not a bad idea for developing body awareness, too. If players persist in running, slow it down to walking, or ask players to come up with a way to move that slows them down.

Age Level

5 years and older.

Equipment Needed

None. Boundary markers, although these can be improvised.

Location and Space Needed

Indoors or out. Minimum space of 10 by 10 feet (3 by 3 meters), and increase slightly for more players. The idea is to keep the area small and a bit crowded so that players keep away from the It partner by using other players to create obstacles. It also makes it harder to run.

Developmental Skills

Primary: adaptability, spontaneity, reaction, visual ability, self-control. Secondary: tactile contact, endurance, cooperation, speed.

Rotation Baseball

Number of Players

4 to 50+.

When to Play the Game

Any time in the middle of a games session. Not normally a first or last game.

Description of Game

Baseball is a lot of fun if you are involved in the action—pitching, hitting, or fielding and throwing. In this game, at least one of these is guaranteed for every player every play! Nobody notices how much or little skill you have—everybody is too busy playing. So, if you feared playing baseball at any time in your life, but you always wanted to play, here is a game for you.

The group is divided into groups of four players who take on four roles: catcher, batter, pitcher, and fielder. If a few groups have five, have two fielders. Groups can be arranged so that they are next and parallel to each other about 10 feet (3 meters) apart.

The batter stands beside the home base and swings the bat at a ball thrown from the pitcher, who is at the other base. The pitcher is trying to make pitches that can be hit, since the batter is up until he or she does hit the ball. Once the batter hits the ball, he or she goes back and forth between the two bases counting each time he or she touches a base as a run.

All of the fielders must touch the ball. Whoever gets the ball must throw it to the other fielders, who throws it to the catcher. The catcher tags home plate,

and the batter is out. After that, everyone rotates positions (for instance, batter becomes fielder, fielder becomes pitcher, pitcher becomes catcher, and catcher becomes batter) and do the same thing again. Everyone gets to play all positions.

While the object is to see who can score the most runs, there is so much commotion with players changing roles that not too much attention is given to who got how many and who did not. So, even if you were terrible at playing baseball, there is an excellent chance you can enjoy this game, and might even get better at some of the skills in the process. What's that? You say you're a cricket fan? More or less the same rules apply, except the terms change (pitcher becomes bowler, home plate become stumps).

Safety Instructions

Use a ball that is soft and large to avoid pain when catching the ball or getting hit by it.

Age Level

5 years and older.

Equipment Needed

A bat, ball, and two bases for every four or five players, though the bases can be improvised. The ball should be soft and large. High-bounce 8-inch-diameter (20 cm) foam balls are great for this. For youngest players, a larger ball may be needed, such as a beach ball, and it may be good to also use a large oversized plastic bat.

Location and Space Needed

Indoors or out, a large space is required. If indoors, a gym is needed. The game is best played outdoors. The groups of four can be next to each other, at least 10 feet (3 meters) apart.

Developmental Skills

Primary: skillfulness and coordination, running, catching, throwing, visual ability, speed, cooperation, self-control. Secondary: problem solving, reaction, verbal contact, endurance, spontaneity.

Serve It Up

Number of Players

5 to 50.

When to Play the Game

Great opening game. Could be used at other times.

Description of Game

A warm-up game is difficult to come by. Such a game will, ideally, make every-one feel included and no one threatened from a game that involves too much physical contact or that is too silly to start with. This game does not call for physical contact, although it will usually happen incidentally, and one does not have to do anything goofy to play. It could even be used at the end to put equipment away.

What happens is very simple. After the leader signals the start, one person takes objects (Frisbees, soft balls, stuffed animals, and the like) from a designated area such as an equipment bag or inside a hula hoop and tosses them around the area. The player takes care not to hit anyone. The group's task is to retrieve the objects and return them to the bag or hoop. Objects must be returned one at a time, and they may not be thrown or passed to another player. Ask a volunteer to count how many objects are retrieved. This goes on for only a minute or so, with someone counting to see how many objects have been returned.

When played again, the group can see if it can increase the number of things returned for the time period chosen. Come to think of it, this might be a good way to get kids to help clean up, while you get to make the mess!

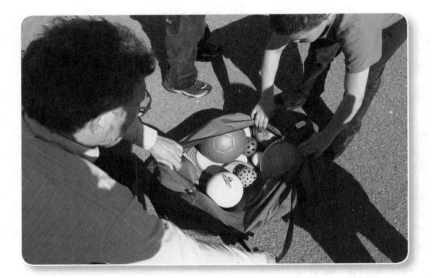

Safety Instructions

Use objects that will not hurt anyone, such as foam balls, stuffed animals, and soft Frisbees. Also, require the one throwing to take care when throwing so as not to hit other players. If no one in the group can do this, you, the leader, need to be the one doing the throwing.

Age Level

5 years and older.

Equipment Needed

An equipment bag, hula hoop, or something that players can return things to; foam balls, stuffed animals, Frisbees, and other soft objects.

Location and Space Needed

Indoors or out. Plenty of room is needed, at least 30 by 30 feet (9 by 9 meters).

Developmental Skills

Primary: self-control, spontaneity, visual ability, skillfulness and coordination, running, speed. Secondary: problem solving, verbal contact, reaction, throwing, catching.

Ultimate Foam Ball

Number of Players

5 to 35.

When to Play the Game

Any time in the middle or end of a session.

Description of Game

This is a game with two teams that looks like a bit of football, basketball, and soccer. In fact, it's Ultimate Frisbee, without the Frisbee. The game is played on a rectangular field with two sidelines and end zones. The object for a team is to advance the foam ball so that it may be caught in its own end zone, which should be at least 10 feet (3 meters) wide.

To start, one team gets on the end of the field that they are defending and throw or kick the ball to the other team on the opposite end of the field. Either team's players can go anywhere on the field, but must keep at least an arm's length distance away from each other. The team with the object or ball cannot run with it; they must advance or move the ball only by passing it to a team-mate. However, they lose possession of the ball if it touches the ground or is intercepted by the opposite team. Once a team scores, they return to the end of the field they are defending and repeat the start by kicking or throwing the ball or object to the other team.

The advantage of playing with a foam ball is that nobody is much of an expert at throwing it—players are all a bit nerdy . . . or is it Nerfy?

Safety Instructions

If players are too aggressive, make the distance the defense players have to keep between themselves and offensive players two or more arm lengths. This should help reduce rough contact.

Age Level

8 years and older.

Equipment Needed

A foam ball or another object that can be easily thrown: foam disc, paper wad, water balloon, for instance. A Frisbee is not used because not all people can throw properly, but most can throw these objects satisfactorily. Boundary markers are very helpful.

Location and Space Needed

Indoors or out, but in any case a large space to allow movement, 50 by 30 feet minimum (15 by 9 meters). For handicapped, very young, and very old players, much less space is needed.

Developmental Skills

Primary: cooperation, verbal contact, adaptability, self-control, reaction, running, throwing and catching. Secondary: problem solving, tactile contact, spontaneity, visual ability, skillfulness and coordination, speed, endurance, jumping.

Wink

Number of Players

10 to 35.

When to Play the Game

Not a game to start with, but one to do late in a session after doing other preliminary trust games. Could be an ending game.

Description of Game

Most times a wink means that a person is flirting or possibly giving a friendly recognition. It could mean either, both, or, most likely, neither of those things in this game.

Players get a partner, and then get in a circle. Pairs are evenly spaced around the circle. One partner is in front of the other while both sit cross legged or kneel. Both are facing the middle forming an inner and outer circle. One person in the circle does not have a partner. She can wink at one of the people in the inner circle.

The person winked at immediately tries to make his way to the winker, but his partner behind him tries to hold on to him for a count of 15. There is no standing; both remain on their hands and knees. Everyone else can help count. If the person winked at manages to make it to the winker and touch them, then he or she stays with the winker, going in back of him or her as the new partner, and the old partner goes back to their starting spot and becomes the new winker. If the winked-at person doesn't make it, he returns with his partner to their spot but changes places so he is now in back of his partner. The game then continues with the winker trying someone new.

The partner behind must start with her hands behind her, to give the person winked at a chance at getting away. When one person who has been winked at does not make it to the winker, the winker can immediately wink at someone else in the inner circle. While this could cause a person to be accused of being a flirt, I doubt it will.

Safety Instructions

This can be a very vigorous game. Before playing, ask players to remove sharp objects that could hurt others, like jagged rings and jewelry, belt buckles, and pens in shirt pockets. Players need to know that if they choose not to play, that is all right. The main rule to go by for playing Wink is that each player does

not try so hard that they hurt the other player. If players can't seem to do this, you can change the game so that a mere tag from the player in back will keep the winked-at person from escaping.

Age Level

8 years and older. Younger players may be able to do this game, but it may be too complicated for some. Size and strength are matched by reaction and speed.

Equipment Needed

If played indoors, mats or carpeting is essential. The version that requires only a tag can be played with the inner circle seated on chairs and the outer circle standing behind them. Or if chairs are not available, all can stand.

Location and Space Needed

For the crawling version, a soft surface such as mats, carpeting, or grass.

Developmental Skills

Primary: tactile contact, self-control, reaction, visual ability, crawling, strength, leaning on. Secondary: speed, verbal contact, skillfulness and coordination, adaptability, endurance, climbing.

Trust Activities

You are probably wondering why these games are not included in the main groupings with the other ones in the game finder. The reason is that these games require a much higher degree of trust (and trustworthiness!) among participants than any of those described earlier. Normally, you need to do other games first to relax the group, and then do some preliminary trust games to build trust levels before attempting any of these games. Very few groups will start out with that degree of trust already established. Depending on the group, some participants might be ready from the start for some of the games in this chapter. This would be the exception. Others might be ready late in the first session, or it could take a year of sessions before the group is ready. And a few groups may never be mature enough for any of these games. You must be the judge. You must know your group and what they are ready for.

How to Judge Readiness

If your group is not able to do the preliminary trust games, they are letting you know that they are not ready for the games presented here. If you start one of these games and see that your group is not ready, that's okay. Just stop the activity and start another one. We all learn by doing. I hope you will not take this advice lightly, because ignoring it could result in an injury. That would be sad, and it is unnecessary. By first doing games that require less trust, you should be able to build the trust level of the group until they can handle the activities in this chapter. These games can deepen the level of assurance among group members.

These games can work when there are people of various sizes in a group. This may be children and adults together or all adults of varied sizes. People who feel self-conscious about their weight find this to be a very good experience because they feel supported physically. It's also good for those who tend not to feel powerful enough to support someone larger than themselves. However, be cautious. If handled incorrectly, these games could be traumatic both physically and emotionally.

I have suggested specific details in each of the games where appropriate, but a general note would be to include assessing the maturity of the group and the degree of trust built up. Go slowly and do not go further than the group can manage or you as the leader can manage. If in doubt, don't do a game; but if you do and it works, it can be a powerful experience.

I want to re-emphasize that if you present the game and you can see it's not working, either stop it and move on to something else, or point out to the group that the way they are doing it is not safe and ask the group what could be done to make it safer. As I've been pointing out throughout the book, this gives the group ownership of the idea, and they will be more likely to respect their own rule. If they don't and the game does not look safe, stop it and try something that requires less trust.

Aura

Activity Level

Low.

Number of Players

2 to 50+.

When to Play the Game

More in the middle of a session when a rest is needed.

Description of Game

I cannot see you, but I know you are there! I can feel your presence as yet undiscovered. Everyone can develop a sensitivity to his or her own aura and the auras from other people. Here is a little activity whereby you can start to develop this sensing.

First, have everyone get a partner. Have them stand facing each other about 3 feet (1 meter) apart with their hands extended toward each other but not quite touching. With your eyes open, try to get a sense of the energy of the other person, and then try it with eyes closed. Move your hands farther and closer to see how that feels.

Finally, when you are both aware of each other's energy (you might get a warm or tingly sensation) with eyes closed, verbally acknowledge it ("Okay, I feel it") and then both turn around three times in the place where you are standing. When you sense you have completed the three turns without talking, reach out slowly to see if you can relocate each other just by sensing the other person. Open your eyes after you feel you have located each other without touching to see how close you have come to making contact. You may be surprised how accurate you are.

Safety Instructions

Some people might find this activity a bit strange if they have never experienced anything like it. They do not have to participate, of course, as long as they do not make others feel self-conscious or disrupt their activity. It probably would make sense to be someplace where other people cannot see the group so as to not make players self conscious.

Age Level

Teens or younger players may not appreciate this activity, so you need to consider their maturity or willingness to try something different before introducing Aura. Then again, they may like it *because* it's different.

Equipment Needed

None.

Location and Space Needed

Any quiet place with enough space for partners in the group to turn around.

Developmental Skills

Primary: cooperation, self-control, balance.

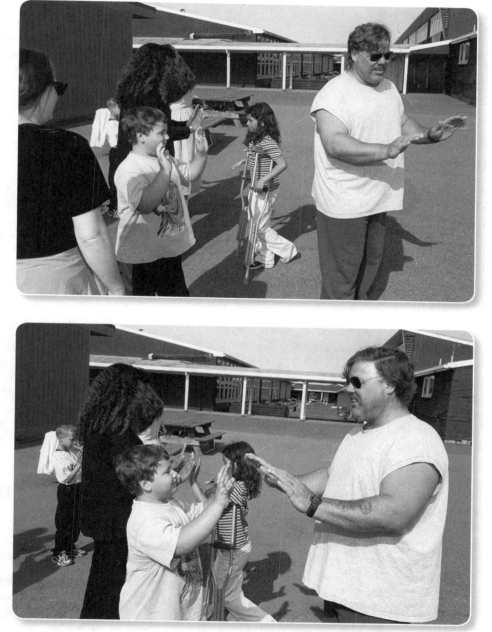

Blind Run

Activity Level

Moderate.

Number of Players

9 to 21. For more than 21 players, form more than one line as needed after demonstrating the game.

When to Play the Game

At or near the end of a session.

Description of Game

Talk about taking a blind dash into the unknown! Although the actual distance covered by a blind runner is usually only about 25 feet or so, with eyes closed, it seems like a long, long way. Most people are absolutely convinced they have gone past the end of the safety lines before they even reach the middle.

To set up this activity, form two parallel lines facing each other, about 6 feet (2 meters) apart. Players stand in their lines at least two arms' lengths apart. Once the lines are formed and people are paying attention, a person on one end of the lines runs between the lines from one end to the other with his eyes closed. The two people at the end where the runner winds up take care to let the runner know he has come to the end of the line by gently tapping him on the shoulder or hip, and, if the runner continues, saying the word *stop*. This is especially important if done indoors or where there are obstacles and walls. The end people should not try to forcibly stop the runner, because it may injure the runner or the stoppers.

The leader demonstrates the game to start, and, before each runner, checks to see that the people at the end of the line who are stopping the person are ready and paying attention. For a second or third turn, runners can spin around before

running and periodically during the whole run. Especially in these two cases, people on the sides must be paying attention in order to avoid being run into and must have their hands ready to guide the runner back into the middle when the runner goes astray, which often happens.

Safety Instructions

This game is safe, provided players are paying close attention. Do not let new runners start before both the line and especially the people on the end are ready. When runners are spinning and a bit dizzy, they tend to run in a crooked path. Therefore, the people in the line must be focused on the runner or possibly be crashed into! No need to worry that a dizzy runner will have enough momentum to do any serious damage, though; I have yet to see the person who could spin and then run quickly!

Sometimes immature players think it is funny to trip the blind runner. But in my experience this does not happen—even with kids—if you as leader make sure everyone knows you are there watching the proceedings. There is a slight risk of a problem if you as leader demonstrate the game first. You can counteract this by having a trustworthy person watch for you while you demonstrate, or if that is not possible, peek a little to avoid being tripped. Of course, if the group is too immature, do not do the game. As with all the games in this chapter, be sure you have established a high degree of trust by doing plenty of preliminary trust games before presenting this one.

Age Level

Age 8 or over. Younger players may need closer watching to see that they don't trip the runner and to stop them at the end of the line.

Equipment Needed

None.

Location and Space Needed

Indoors or outdoors. If done indoors, it should be in a large room where there is room for the line to spread out. Make very sure the runner knows when she reaches the end of the line so she does not crash into a wall, even if it means yelling, "Stop!"

Developmental Skills

Primary: balance, skillfulness and coordination, cooperation. Secondary: tactile contact, running, adaptability, self-control, speed.

Body Surfing (or Log Roll)

Activity Level

Moderate.

Number of Players

10 to 50+. For every 15 to 20 players, make another line of "waves."

When to Play the Game

The end of a session.

Description of Game

Let's go surfin'! All right, so you do not have an ocean or a lake or even a river. You might not even have a stream. It doesn't matter. In this activity, we use people for our waves. This isn't such a drawback—even the Beach Boys couldn't surf, save one.

Get players, "waves," to lie facedown, in a line and parallel, about 1 foot (30 centimeters) apart. Make sure small players are placed between two larger ones so that the smaller ones do not take too much weight from the larger surfers. Have one player, the "surfer," kneel and then lie perpendicularly across with arms outstretched on top of and in the middle of the waves at one end of the line. Be sure to have plenty of space on the opposite end of the line so that the waves have somewhere to go. Have the waves that the surfer touches start to roll, thus propelling the surfer down the line.

As waves roll into other waves, they start to roll, too. The surfer is transported down the line to the other end, where a "lifeguard" or two can help the surfer off of the waves without making it too painful for the waves. If the surfer goes off the middle of the line, these helpers can guide the surfer back to the middle. Once a surfer reaches the end of the line, have a person at the head of the line become the new surfer. The line of waves may have to move back to their original starting spot to create enough room.

Safety Instructions

If the surfer starts rolling off the center of the waves, she should be encouraged to move back to the middle. As a facilitator, you can physically assist her if necessary. It can be rather painful if the surfer gets all her weight on the other players' legs, and it can be a little too personal if the surfer gets up around the chest and face area. Also, before the next surfer starts, make sure that there is room for her to surf across the whole line in the given space. The line may have to move, or the surfer could start on the opposite side of the line and surf back. If your group is on a lawn, check to see (you can ask the group to help) that it's not wet or has prickly plants, sticks, glass, or animal droppings.

Age Level

Generally, 18 years and older. However, a mature group of younger children can handle it. In a group of mixed ages, the children should be fit in between adults so as not to take the full weight of the surfer.

Equipment Needed

If indoors, this should be done on a soft surface such as mats or carpeting. If outdoors, on grass. I would not do it on cement or blacktop.

Location and Space Needed

Indoors or out, but on a soft surface. Enough room so that a surfer can surf the length of the line of players (about 1.5 times the length of the line).

Developmental Skills

Primary: cooperation, trust, tactile contact, self-control, leaning on. Secondary: problem solving, verbal contact, adaptability, spontaneity, skillfulness and coordination, climbing, pantomime.

Greeting Game

Activity Level
Low/moderate.

Number of Players
5 to 50.

When to Play the Game
A group is not ready for this game unless they are ready for *anything*, highly relaxed, and dressed in casual clothes.

Description of Game
I can safely say that players will never have been greeted by old friends, much less total strangers, in ways that they will be in this game. It's outrageous, it's audacious, it's a blast! And all from a simple greeting.

To start, players get down on their hands and knees. They can then begin to greet one another in unconventional ways without using words. However, sounds and touch are allowed and encouraged! For instance, a person may crawl to another player, turn over on his back, wiggle his arms and legs in the air, and say, "Blub-blub." The other player might raise her upper body, start bobbing her head and arms, and reply, "Ooga-ooga." The only limits are the players' imaginations and common decency. Here is a chance to be completely spontaneous, and almost anything goes! It is vital that you demonstrate a greeting or two to give them the idea.

Safety Instructions
For a group that is reserved or nervous about participating, this is probably not a good choice, although no one makes anyone do anything weird. Players

can always do some very mild greeting that will not embarrass them or the person being greeted. It would certainly make sense to do some preliminary trust games before this one. But for a group that has gotten into the spirit of play to some degree, this game is a good way to take them a step further. You may need to remind players (middle school age and older) that inappropriate touching is not okay, especially if you notice it happening. ("Keep it decent!")

Age Level

All.

Equipment Needed

None.

Location and Space Needed

Preferably a soft surface such as grass, carpet, or mat. It is best played out of public view to avoid embarrassment.

Developmental Skills

Primary: spontaneity, crawling, creativity, adaptability, problem solving. Secondary: cooperation, pantomime, climbing, leaning on, strength, visual ability, skillfulness and coordination, reaction, tactile contact.

Trust Leap

Activity Level

High.

Number of Players

9 to 20. With more players, make two groups.

When to Play the Game

This game should be done only after quite a few preliminary games and, especially, other trust exercises have been done. A definite strong bond of trust needs to be established before attempting this activity, so leave it until later in a session. It's important to be aware of what your group can handle. If they can, this game is exhilarating.

Description of Game

Divide the players into groups of at least nine, and have each group form two parallel lines facing one another 3 feet (1 meter) apart. Make sure that children or small people are *not* placed opposite or next to one another, especially in the area where the person's head should land when he leaps into the group's waiting arms. Place larger and stronger players in the middle of the line to support weight. Each person holds out both arms, alternating each arm with one of

the arms of the person across from him or her. They should not hold on to one another because this strains the wrists too much. Each person in the line is close to the next person, nearly touching. There are no gaps. Strongly suggest that players in the line bend their legs a bit to absorb the weight of the person they catch. Also, make sure everyone has their head back so they don't get hit.

The leader demonstrates how the game is done by taking a running leap into the group's arms. The best way to jump is with arms extended out in front. This will distribute the weight out more evenly so that there is less stress on the catchers. Then others in the group take turns doing the same. Each time before the person takes a run and leap, she needs to ask if the group is ready; or if she doesn't, the leader must. Later on, perhaps even on another day, the group can fall into the arms of the group from varying heights, up to 6 feet (2 meters).

Safety Instructions

To repeat, make sure that two children or small people are not placed opposite or next to each other, especially in the area where the person's head and trunk should land when he leaps into the group's waiting arms. The group must absolutely pay attention so that there are no mishaps. If you as the leader notice the attention of a person wandering, stop the activity and simply get the person's attention back to the task of catching the next person. You can do this in a manner that does not embarrass anyone but simply helps people refocus, like asking, "Are you ready?" This is a safe activity when players are paying attention. This game is best done on a soft surface.

Age Level

15 years and older. Younger players can do this game, but with them you must be extra cautious as you evaluate their readiness and prepare them with preliminary trust activities. It may take hours, days, weeks, months, or in some cases even years before some groups are ready for the responsibility that this game requires. I am not exaggerating. You must evaluate the readiness of your group. Now, having scared you, when the group is focused and ready, this game is invigorating.

Equipment Needed

None.

Location and Space Needed

Wherever the game is played, it is highly desirable to do so on a soft surface such as on mats or grass. There must be enough room for a person to run and leap into the line, at least 15 feet (about 5 meters).

Developmental Skills

Primary: tactile contact, self-control, cooperation, visual ability, strength. Secondary: running, jumping, verbal contact, adaptability.

Trust Lift

Activity Level

High.

Number of Players

8 minimum; make another group to lift for every 8 players. If you have an awkward number, say 12 people, then take turns having a few sit out for a few people who get lifted, especially the person just lifted—to give him or her a chance to enjoy it.

When to Play the Game

Usually near the end of a session or after a series of sessions, depending on the trust built up within the group. As with any of these high-trust games, do some preliminary trust games before attempting these.

Description of Game

Divide the group into at least 8 players (but no more than 10) each, and ask one in each group to volunteer to be lifted. The volunteer lies down and closes his eyes while the rest of the group members gather around, placing their hands on him. Make sure that stronger and larger players are around the trunk of the person being lifted and that one lifter will support the person's head. For about a half minute, the group gets in synch with the volunteer's breathing, then they put their hands under him and begin slowly to lift using their legs (not their backs!) until the volunteer is over the heads of the group. While they have the person in the air, the group can turn around slowly in a circle.

Then they slowly bring the person down to waist level and begin to rock back and forth while continuing to slowly lower the person gently to the ground. The group again places their hands on the volunteer for another half minute before moving away. If there are enough people in the group, the person just lifted can sit out a turn to enjoy the effects and watch someone else being lifted.

Safety Instructions

If someone does not want to be lifted, do not insist that they be lifted. That doesn't mean that you cannot try to coax someone, but, as always, respect a player's right to say no. Also, to reinforce a point, make absolutely certain someone tall enough is supporting the volunteer's head, which will protect the person's neck and spine.

Insist that those lifting do so with their legs, not with their backs. This means they will have to bend their legs and keep their backs straight. To repeat, I recommend that players do some preliminary trust games before this one.

It's not very funny to the person being lifted to hear someone say, "Let's drop her!" or, even worse, to actually be dropped. All trust within the group is lost. It also is dangerous if even one person lets her attention wander. Everyone needs to be present. Your job as leader is to keep the group focused and discourage negative comments beforehand. Then the game is safe.

Age Level

15 years and older. Younger players can do this, but as leader you must be sure that the attitude of the group is sincere and focused.

Equipment Needed

None.

Location and Space Needed

Just enough clear space is needed so that the group can lift a person, turn around, and let the person down. A soft surface is desirable.

Developmental Skills

Primary: strength, cooperation, tactile contact. Secondary: self-control, skillfulness and coordination, balance, verbal contact.

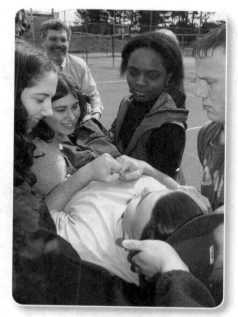

Willow in the Wind (or Trust Circle)

Activity Level

Moderate.

Number of Players

7 to 50; with 13 or more players, make two circles (or as many as needed) after demonstrating.

When to Play the Game

Do some preliminary trust games or spotting activities before this activity. This is especially true for kids or people who act like kids.

Description of Game

This game is borrowed from the human potential movement a long while back, but, hey, who's keeping score?

A group of 6 to 12 people form a circle, standing around a person who stands in the middle with his arms crossed in front of him and his hands on opposite shoulders. He remains straight but relaxed, with feet together. Those in the circle have hands up and ready to catch, with legs slightly bent, one leg forward and one back, braced to catch the one in the middle, using their legs to take the weight. To start, the circle should be close to the middle person so that the person feels safe and so that it is safe.

The person in the middle allows himself to fall straight back and is gently caught and passed by people in the circle. He should try to keep his legs straight and feet together and, if he wants to, he can close his eyes. Depending on how well the group is able to support the person and how comfortable the person feels, he can stop and ask the supporters to move farther away (say, each person can move 6 inches back), which will make it a bit more exciting, or closer to the person, which will feel safer. Moving closer can also work well if the person in the middle is very tall or large. After a minute or so, change the middle person.

Willow in the Wind (or Trust Circle)

Safety Instructions

A significant amount of trust has to be built up in the group before attempting this activity, and it is not a good activity to start with unless the group is very cohesive and mature. It is important that the circle give complete attention to the middle person; as leader, you must focus yourself and keep the group focused. This point cannot be emphasized enough. Dropping someone is bad enough, but if the person is hurt, the game is over. No one will trust the rest of the group after that.

Age Level

15 years and older. Younger players can do this but typically need verbal and practical preparation with less demanding trust games first.

Equipment Needed

None.

Location and Space Needed

Indoors or out. An open space is required for the group to be able to make the circles required for the activity. A soft surface is desirable.

Developmental Skills

Primary: tactile contact, cooperation, strength, self-control, leaning on, verbal contact, adaptability.

Afterword

A merry heart doeth good like a medicine.
—Bible: Proverbs

When I was 30, my mother died, the house I lived in was sold (meaning that everyone living in it would have to move out), my source of income dried up, and the project I'd been working on for a year fell apart. All within a month. At that point, all I could do was laugh. After all, what else could go wrong? Then I sat around for several weeks simply because I had no energy to do anything, and I was all right with that.

During that period, I had been scheduled to do a New Games presentation at a psychiatric day care center. I was able to postpone the session. When I decided that the time had come to resume my life, I rescheduled the games session. When I arrived at the day care center, one of the participants told me that one of the clients who was supposed to be there had committed suicide just days earlier. Everyone was upset. For me, it was the last straw. When it came time to lead the session, all I could do was sit there. I just didn't have the motivation to get up. For the first and only time in my life presenting New Games, I could not even move. It seemed like 5 minutes went by, although it was probably more like 30 seconds. Finally, one of the clients asked, "Are we gonna play some games?" My reply was "I hope so." The realization that someone really wanted to do New Games was enough to get me going. At last, I was able to get up.

I suggested we go to the park across the street for the games. Everyone agreed, and what followed was one of the most ecstatic games sessions I have ever led. For that period, I not only forgot that I was grieving, but I forgot all the other problems that had surfaced as well. The group was able to forget their grief, too. The only thing we were aware of was playing in the park together and having fun. It was all that mattered. Having that little breather from pain was as healing for me as it was for them.

How did that little breather from pain happen? I think it was because we all got very much in the present (that is, incidentally, the goal of meditation). The point of New Games is to focus on the present and find happiness. If you follow this principle in other aspects of life, the ramifications are immense. Say you are unhappy in your job, relationship, or any other aspect of your life. Do you stick with what you've got for security, out of fear of the unknown, or just because you think things are the best that you deserve? It might not mean giving something up, but it will usually mean making some changes.

Know the true value of time, snatch, seize and enjoy every
moment of it.
—Lord Chesterfield

I believe that if you are not happy in the present, you need to look at what will make you happy and then take action and live by that action. By focusing on what makes you happy in a given situation, by being true to yourself and then doing what makes you happy, you will become a happier person. The important thing is to focus on what you feel will make you happy, not what you think will. By finding joy in the present during play, you find a way of practicing this. New Games become a metaphor for life. Not only do they give you good feelings for the moment, but they also carry over to the next thing you do by changing your outlook, thereby helping you keep those positive feelings.

By the way, I have found that beyond the amount of money required for survival, more money has not made me any happier. Neither have more gadgets and material possessions, though I do have some of these for work and pleasure. New Games do make me happy in the moment, though there is more to deep and long-lasting happiness that can be known as well. But that is beyond the scope of this book. Suffice it to say that it relates to spiritual awareness.

Also, letting go of your fears and apprehensions about trying something different in New Games is a good analogy to apply to life. Take a chance. What is the worst that can happen? You might make a mistake? Learn from it, but don't let it stop you from trying, if it feels right in your heart.

Dale N. Le Fevre

Following are other related educational materials by Dale N. Le Fevre:

DVDs

Complete Cooperative New Games

New Parachute Games

Best of New Games

Best of Cooperative Games

Books

Parachute Games With DVD (coauthored with Todd Strong, published by Human Kinetics)

The Spirit of Play

CD-ROM

New Games CD-ROM, Revised

For information on these materials, seminars, and a workshop schedule, see the New Games website or contact Dale at the following site:

www.iNewGames.com

E-mail: dale@inewgames.com

About the Author

When I was born I was so surprised I couldn't talk for a year and a half.

—*Gracie Allen*

Dale N. Le Fevre started working with the nonprofit New Games Foundation (NGF) in 1975 as a volunteer. By the start of 1976 he was office manager and associate director. In 1977 he formed his own project, Play Express, which took New Games into schools, while he continued to give trainings for the NGF. In 1979 he left the United States for eight years to promote New Games worldwide.

To date, Le Fevre has conducted over 1,000 New Games workshops worldwide. His workshop participants have included Jews and Arabs in Israel in the early '80s; mixed races in apartheid-era South Africa; Protestants and Catholics in Northern Ireland in the early '80s and late '90s; and Croats, Serbs, and Muslims in Croatia and Serbia in '93, '94, and '98.

Le Fevre's publications include *The Spirit of Play* (previously published in five languages) and *Parachute Games With DVD,* coauthored with Todd Strong (Human Kinetics). He also produced several DVDs, including *Complete Cooperative New Games, Best of New Games, Best of Cooperative Games,* and *New Parachute Games.* He also produced the *New Games CD-ROM, Revised.*

Most recently, Le Fevre has founded a new company, Playworks, which works with businesses to use New Games to help resolve conflict, improve communication, build stronger teams, and reduce stress.

Le Fevre holds an MA in education from New York University and a BS in business from Valparaiso University, Indiana. In his free time he enjoys gardening, hiking, biking, dancing, and camping. He lives in Sheffield, England.

You'll find other outstanding
games resources at
www.HumanKinetics.com

In the U.S. call 1.800.747.4457
Australia 08 8372 0999
Canada. 1.800.465.7301
Europe . . . . . +44 (0) 113 255 5665
New Zealand 0800 222 062

HUMAN KINETICS
The Information Leader in Physical Activity
P.O. Box 5076 • Champaign, IL 61825-5076